TEAM

TEAM

JOHN VOGEL

MELISSA MATHEWS SHIMP

LUMINARE PRESS

WWW.LUMINAREPRESS.COM

Cover Design by Melissa K. Thomas

Luminare Press
442 Charnelton St.
Eugene, OR 97401
www.luminarepress.com

LCCN: 2020925752
ISBN: 978-1-64388-573-5

This book is dedicated to every swimmer, coach, and parent that has ever been a part of TEAM. The commitment from every person I have had the privilege to work with over the course of my career is what made TEAM a successful combination of Winning, Oneness, and Family.

CONTENTS

JOHN VOGEL

John Vogel on the pool deck during 1980's

John began his swimming career for the Shamrock Hilton Swim Club in 1961. He won many Texas Age Group Swimming (TAGS) championships, set many state records, and contributed to championship team wins as an age group swimmer. John attended Memorial High School where the team won four straight UIL state titles. He then attended the University of Tennessee where he was a four year letterman. John returned to Texas in 1978 to start his coaching career for Meyerland Aquatic Club. He also coached for Space City Aquatics (SCAT) before moving to The Woodlands

Swim Team, where he coached for eighteen years. Combined his teams won twenty-nine TAGS Team Championships, three with SCAT and twenty-six with The Woodlands Swim Team (TWST), he also never lost a US Swimming or High School dual meet or swim off. On a national level, John's teams won seven Junior National Titles, finished in the top ten at Senior Nationals, and had swimmers place in the top eight at three consecutive Olympic Trials. Before retiring, John coached the McCullough High School boys team to a UIL state title, and was voted district, regional, and state coach of the year. After retiring from TWST, John owned and operated The Swim Shops of the Southwest while also managing over twenty TISCA high school coaching clinics. Currently, John has delivered several speaking engagements or clinics for many U.S. swim teams with TEAM being the central theme. He also gives private swim lessons for serious and highly competitive swimmers swimming for various teams. He lives with his wife Gail in Houston, has two children, and one grandchild.

MELISSA MATHEWS SHIMP

Melissa started swimming at the age of twelve. She swam at the national level most of her swimming career attending her first Junior National Meet when she was thirteen in Milwaukee, Wisconsin. She was a state finalist several years at the high school level. Melissa earned a scholarship to Texas Christian University. She never swam for John Vogel, but admired the team aspects of The

Woodlands Swim Team. When Melissa was nineteen, her mother Gail married John. She has been chef and owner of her personal chef company for twelve years and is known to bring Gail along on her chef days. She lives in The Woodlands with her husband John and their two daughters.

PROLOGUE

I t was suggested that I write a book on competitive swimming by my first childhood swim coach, Gene Shumway, a Texas Hall of Fame Coach inductee himself. Gene was not only a great coach, but has remained a great friend and huge influence on my life even to this day. Here are a few words from Gene:

I would like to tell you what I know and believe about one of my closest friends, a man I have known since November 1964, Coach John Vogel. I was holding an age group workout at the old Gateway Indoor pool in Houston, Texas when I looked up and saw Coach Phil Hansel leading a woman and a young boy down the deck. He introduced me to Mrs. Toni Vogel and her ten year old son, John. Coach Hansel said Mrs. Vogel would like John to swim for me. With John swimming butterfly, our relay team beat the national champions, The Panther Boys Club out of Little Rock, Arkansas and set the national record. Now as Paul Harvey would say "Here is the rest of the story."

I coached John at the Dad's Club. He was a top age group swimmer, a top Texas high school swimmer and a top collegiate swimmer at the University of Tennessee. Wait, the story gets better. After college, John returned to Houston and began his coaching career. First at Meyerland Country Club, I was impressed with his swimmers. So, when an opening for a coach at SCAT became available, I encouraged him to apply. John became head age group coach and did a wonderful job of building that team. Several years later I was living in The Woodlands, north of Houston and they were looking for someone to take over the job as head coach. I had been working with several swimmers between flying my trips for Continental and knew several people on the search committee. I recommended John for the job. The only problem was John did not want to leave his swimmers at SCAT, which I understood. Coach Phil Hansel once told me, "you need three things to have a successful swim program, a coach, a program, and a pool." John had two of the three [ed. He didn't have the pool], but at The Woodlands he would have it all. At The Woodlands, John produced age group, high school, junior and senior national champions. He won the Texas High School Championship, and twenty-nine Texas Aquatic Swimming Championships. A coach often becomes known for a swimmer, but I believe the true greatness is a coach who builds his team, wins championships, and most of all, makes each swimmer proud of their accomplishments. John Vogel, in my opinion, has excelled at this like no other. I have encouraged John to write this book. Why? It is because I love the sport of competitive swimming. I see many coaches and swimmers take from the sport and not give back to the sport. What John Vogel has to say is important to my sport. Read it, study it, and use it.

—GENE SHUMWAY
Age Group Coach and Texas
Swimming Hall of Fame Inductee

*A view of The Woodlands Athletic Center
from the ten meter diving platform.*

A NOTE FROM JOHN:

I thought for months about how to approach this task. I wanted this book to be different from current publications on the market. Mainly, I will be talking about TEAM, the culture that I try to instill in all my swimmers. I will not be addressing stroke technique as many others have already covered that subject. Although technique is a very important part of swimming, it is not the only part of being successful. I will, however, touch on some other technical parts of a successful swim program.

One aspect of the sport of swimming I have not seen discussed too often is winning as a team and how winning as a team contributes to being the best swimmer you can be. Most people do not think of swimming as a team sport, but surprisingly swimming has all the components of team sports. Swimmers race individual events and relays and earn points towards a team total. The individuals must come together as a team much like football, baseball, or track and field.

The TEAM culture applies to business, as well. I used TEAM at Swim Shops with my employees. I challenged them to think as a team, putting the business and their co-workers on the same level as their own personal goals.

If I help you become a better swimmer, athlete, coach, or swim parent then I have accomplished my goal. I believe in three great things: God, Family, and Team. Be the best you can be.

Enjoy,
Coach John
~~AAA0~~

INTRODUCTION

During my coaching career I chose an unorthodox way of approaching success—TEAM. I focused on building a team culture instead of focusing solely on the individual swimmer. I believe the individual swimmer achieves more success by being part of a bigger picture, a successful team. By promoting and nurturing a team mindset I believe both the individual swimmer and team is more successful.

This unique approach is used by many teams who have achieved success. I have seen many collegiate teams adopt this approach, yet very few USA swimming teams. The University of Texas Swim Team under Coach Eddie Reese, University of Tennessee with Coach Matt Kredich, University of Georgia coached by Jack Bauerle are some examples of collegiate teams. The Woodlands Swim Team, Mission Viejo, and Ft. Lauderdale under Coach Jack Nelson are great examples of USA swim teams that have achieved success using a team culture.

The greatest team we all witness is the U.S. Olympic team. Should we not follow their example and create our own team environments? Wearing team uniforms or warm ups, participating in cheering for every swimmer during races, and supporting each other in and out of the pool are just a few examples of how to grow the team mentality.

TEAM is a family of coaches, swimmers, and parents working together to foster a strong team bond. TEAM takes everyone striving every day in and out of the pool to keep each other motivated for success. TEAM starts at the top with the coach leading the way, much like the CEO of a business, to innovate and inspire athletes to be the best they can be together. As a coach I believe nurturing a TEAM mentality will lead to success for not only the team but especially the individual swimmer as well.

> I have watched John's teams for years. To a person, the best group of racers I've seen. To be the best you can be, in any sport, you must compete. In swimming, you must race. This book will make you better.

—EDDIE REESE
Head Men's Coach University of Texas
and Multi-Olympic Head Coach

A young John during his freshman year at the University of Tennessee

Chapter 1

"ONENESS"

During my swimming career I was fortunate to swim for great teams with strong team environments. Not until my freshman year at the University of Tennessee under the direction of men's head coach, Ray Bussard had I ever heard the word "Oneness," much less understood what it meant. Coach Bussard would later become an U.S. Olympic Coach. Boy, I could never have imagined how one word, "Oneness," would affect my entire coaching career or life.

My freshman year we had just swam our annual orange and white intersquad meet. I was on cloud nine because I had just broken the record in the 1650 yard freestyle. We were sitting in the team meeting after the meet when Coach Bussard came into the room and angrily threw his clipboard, a total buzz kill. He was upset because neither the orange nor white team had shown "Oneness" during the meet. Coach Bussard informed "us ladies" just how we were going to learn the meaning of the word "Oneness" with a midnight practice. With scholarships on the line, we had no choice but to comply. Some of us slept at the pool and some went to their dorm rooms, but we were all lined up at midnight for our practice. Looking back now, that may have been the most important practice I had ever swam. At the end of a two hour swim practice, we thought we were done but unfortunately Coach Bussard had other plans. We were told to jump in the diving well, form a circle, and hold hands. This is when we realized this was not just a regular practice. He said during the next exercise if our hands let go we lose our scholarship. He instructed us to rotate the circle by treading water while lifting our arms out of the water and keep rotating. Once we were rolling in one direction we had to change and rotate in the opposite direction. This exercise of rotating the circle went on for forty-five minutes. Next he had us climb out of the pool to do vertical jumps while reaching for a line drawn high on the wall. Then he had us squeeze into a circle he had drawn on the pool deck. We were squeezed in that circle, hot and sweaty, shoulder to shoulder. We then had to run back to the wall, do more vertical jumps and run back to an even smaller circle he had drawn on the pool deck. We somehow managed to squeeze twenty-eight swimmers into this circle, this time we were body to body. Round three, we were back to vertical jumping on the wall and squeezing into an even smaller circle. This circle was so small we could not physically fit into it. In order to fit everyone in the circle, some swimmers were boosted on top of the shoulders of other swimmers. We succeeded! At this point, we were shaking and exhausted. Coach walked over to us and said, "I hope you learned something. See you at practice later today." When practice was over I looked at the clock. It was 6:00 a.m.! I could not believe we had been at the pool all night. Freshman to seniors, all went back to the dorm to sit together and relive the evening. While we were reliving the nightmare workout we had all just endured, we realized we had become a team during practice, and finally understood what Coach Bussard meant by the word "Oneness."

*University of Tennessee boys team at the
2020 Southeast Conference Championships*

During practice that night and later that morning the entire team, from freshman to seniors, bonded like nothing I had ever experienced before. We began to understand what "Oneness" truly meant, and later that season we saw incredible team results. Once the team overcame adversity together as one, great things started to happen. That season the team went undefeated in dual meets, won the Southeast Conference Championship, and went on to place third at the NCAA Championship. Three years later the University of Tennessee won the NCAA National Championships, but more importantly to this day they remain one family. When swimmers believe not only in themselves but in their teammates, a bond is created that lasts long after swimming careers are over. This is the true definition of "Oneness", and for myself it started with that midnight workout. All these years later, the concepts of team and Oneness still drive the University of Tennessee Swim Team.

As a US Navy veteran, I KNOW the importance of being a "Team".

Starting in boot camp, our heads are shaved, we are broken down and stripped of our individuality so that we may begin to know the meaning of the word "Shipmate". Shipmate is what we were to ALWAYS refer to each other during the ensuing arduous weeks. A shipmate is always there at your side and may, one day, be there to save your life, or you for them. I was not a SEAL, not SWCC (Surface Warfare Combatant Crewman), nor was I even stationed aboard a ship…I was a Navy musician. A band, orchestra, or chamber group ALWAYS has to rely on each other to be well prepared for each rehearsal and performance! As they say, "A chain is only as strong as its weakest link", and no one wants to be that link!!!

I've only known John Vogel for a couple years, but I am a very good judge of character and I think VERY highly of John!!! He knows how to motivate a group of kids without demoralizing or coaching by intimidation. Trust me when I say that I have encountered my fair share of those types of coaches and teachers!

One final thought about TEAM is that when morale is high so is performance. When performance is high, so is morale!!! They go hand in hand. Only a real TEAM is capable of this!!!

John, I look forward to reading your book and passing it along to my trumpet students as they will gain a different perspective to why it is so very important to be on time, prepared, and ready to help their "Team Mates" so that they will all succeed!

—MATT JENKINS
Friend and Retired U.S. Navy

SPACE CITY AQUATIC TEAM (SCAT)

When I was hired at SCAT they had just won second place at TAGS, Texas Age Group Swimming State Championship. At the time Dad's Club was the best team in Texas as they had been dominating swimming under the direction of Coaches Richard Quick and Skip Kenny. Richard Quick went on to coach Auburn University, The University of Texas, and Stanford University, winning NCAA Championships at all three universities. Skip Kenny coached at Stanford and also won NCAA Championships as well. Together Richard and Skip coached the Women's and Men's Olympic Swim Team. Needless to say, Dad's Club was definitely looking like the team to beat. As the course of the season went on, we began to realize the team from the City of Plano was actually the stronger team. Everything we had been doing to mentally prepare our swimmers to beat Dad's Club was off base. We, the coaches, had not done the correct preparation by studying well enough what was happening in other parts of the state. Somehow I had to get these swimmers minds in the right place mentally, so I came up with a plan. I called a practice for the entire TAGS team. About half way through our practice, we heard a pounding on the door that led outside. I told my swimmers to let me check who was at the door. When I opened the door, a nicely dressed man in a suit and tie was standing there holding a funeral wreath. I explained to him he must be in the wrong place, but the man insisted he was at the correct location. When I opened the card attached to the wreath, it was signed from the City of Plano Swim Team. I said to the kids "I can't believe an age group team would go to this level. Are you guys going to stand up and fight to prove them wrong?" Well, this just fired up the kids to go out there and beat them at the meet. This act reset the swimmer's minds with a new target. With the kids fired up and $100 out of my pocket for the wreath, the kids were mentally ready to go to the meet. Bringing the whole team together with a common goal is one of the most important aspects of TEAM.

Team picture after Space City Aquatic Team won TAGS in 1980

THE WOODLANDS AND "ONENESS"

After two and half years at SCAT as the age group coach, the team offered me the head coaching position. My first age group swim coach, Gene Shumway informed me that the head coaching position at the Woodlands Swim Team was also available. After much thought I knew what I needed to do. It was hard to leave SCAT, but to further my career I needed to make the jump to a different team. I was offered and accepted the head coaching position at The Woodlands Swim Team.

My first workout as Head Coach did not go as I had planned. The kids were dismissing me as head coach, there was a lack of respect, and I had the impression they were there to just have fun not work hard. This was not the team I had envisioned when taking this position. Then the existing assistant coach showed up on the pool deck making demands of me in front of the team. These were demands I was not willing to compromise the team for, so I fired him immediately in front of the entire team. After witnessing the firing, the kids were shell shocked, but at this point I had their attention. I explained I had prepared a great workout, but instead I decided to go in a different direction. I told the kids if they wanted to stay on the team they were to swim a three thousand meter butterfly instead of the workout I had planned.

I thought to myself after that practice that none of the swimmers would come back and I was going to be fired. To my amazement the following practice every swimmer came back ready to work. It was that practice we began our journey to "Oneness" and becoming a team.

This was just one of my challenges at The Woodlands that first year. I started off with only five TAGS qualifying swimmers and placed thirty-sixth at the state meet that first season. However, by implementing TEAM, we won the state championship two years later.

When I swam at The Woodlands under our coach, John Vogel our goal was to win TAGS each year. The season always started with a team meeting to focus on goal setting. TAGS couldn't be won by an individual, it was won as a team. We were training to do our best, for the benefit and support of the team. We learned to be very competitive, goal-oriented, and focused. We learned what loss felt like, we did not like it. Nowhere was winning more important than on relays. Personally, I loved the competition and camaraderie with pushing each other to be our best that a relay provided. My teammates pushed me to be better. I wanted to be my best for them more than myself. I didn't want to let them down, my team down, or my coach down. As we pushed each other out of our comfort zones, we got better and better. I made some of my best childhood memories and friends on The Woodlands Swim Team. That I will never forget. We are all winners!

Being on The Woodlands Swim Team was so much more than a childhood activity and sport, it taught me life-long lessons I still use today. We were trained to have good work ethic, be good winners, gracious losers, visualize, set goals and be part of a team to always strive to be our best, for ourselves, but more so for the benefit of the whole team.

John's coaching helped us be better swimmers and people. Those traits now make me the person who I am today. Thanks.

—BRADLEY BAILEY
Past Woodlands Swimmer

Chapter 2

THERE IS NO I IN TEAM

The first step to having a successful season was to have a team meeting at the start of every season. This team meeting set expectations and established confidence in each other for the rest of the swim season. We discussed several items in the meeting and held a candle ceremony in which everyone participated. To set the tone for the meeting I would ask the swimmers three questions for contemplation. I asked the swimmers to ponder these questions in their minds. The answers they came up with would be their own and may be different from another swimmer. The swimmers were to expect that I would be able to answer these same questions.

Are you committed to excellence? What are things you do to support your own commitment to excellence? What type of lifestyle do you live which affects this commitment? Things to consider when thinking about this question would be coming to practice prepared to swim fast and committed to the training that will lead to success. Showing up on time everyday prepared to work hard while supporting each other and the team were also another important consideration. The swimmers could rely on the fact I always came to practice on time prepared to help them be the best swimmer they could be.

Can I trust you? The athlete should have confidence in the fact that their coach will make the best decisions for training. Creating challenging workouts for the betterment of the swimmer, training the athlete so not to cause injuries, and making the right decisions on resting and tapering for meets are some of the expectations an athlete should have of the coach. The swimmers also need to have faith their coach will be a source of encouragement and support. The coach should have certainty the athlete will come to practice every day able to communicate any concerns and be willing to work hard. One of the most important ingredients in creating a successful team is trust. The swimmers also need to trust each other. In TEAM, the environment is created so that trust is assured by both athletes, coaches, and parents. Everyone should have confidence that each individual will support the team culture which leads to success.

Do you care about me as a person? I hope that the swimmers cared about me and the others on the team. Cheering and supporting each other were beliefs I instilled in these athletes. Caring for each other as part of TEAM instills interpersonal skills which lasts well beyond swimming careers. When athletes care about the others around them they will be more willing to push themselves to success. At the same time, swimmers have lives outside of swimming. We as coaches have a duty to respect and honor this because outside distractions can and will affect performance. Having the awareness of situations in an athlete's life which may be more important than a swim practice. Parents getting divorced, a car accident, or a loss of a friend or family member are just a couple examples of situations my swimmers faced. Those were the rough days where just being there for them as support was more important than being in the pool. As the case may be just sitting silent with the swimmer and/ or family as a way of support and love as part of TEAM was the right place to be instead of in the pool.

These are meant to have the athletes see that TEAM is greater than swimming on a swim team. TEAM is a support system to inspire everyone to be the best they can be. The questions came from the great football coach and public speaker, Lou Holtz. I find such inspiration in his vision of life and coaching. These questions can apply to anything in life—marriage, business, or sports. These questions definitely drove my way of coaching for the rest of my career and life. I knew I had to incorporate these into my vision of Team. These questions were to help inspire the swimmers into better athletes and human beings. The next item during the team meeting was to elect team captains. I believe incorporating peers as team captains is a part of achieving success as a team. The captains were elected by their peers at the meeting. I feel the role of team captains is so important I dedicate an entire chapter to their role in this book.

Last on the agenda at the meeting we discussed team goals. Once everyone was on board with the team goals, I had the lights turned off and lit my candle. The assistant coaches lit their candle from mine, followed by team captains, the seniors, all the way down to the youngest age group swimmers. All of a sudden the room was brighter than when the lights were turned on. It is then, in that moment, the team started to believe what we could accomplish. Working together and believing in each other, instead of being individuals caring only for ourselves we became Team. Starting with just one light in the dark, one by one as a team we came together and lit the room. The swimmers began to see "Oneness" as the key ingredient to the team's success.

Building a great team culture is the most important thing we do as coaches. It's more important than any strategy or workout plan we may have. Coaches spend an incredible amount of time strategizing, but I am constantly reminding myself, a team's culture is most important. I've heard it said before that a team's culture is what determines if any strategy will actually work. I believe that. At A&M, we talk a lot about 'TEAMWORK'. That's what we want our culture to be built on. That's our catch-phrase. It's on our workout caps, it's talked about, preached about, and stressed a lot. We want our team to figure out how to work together. Most times it's not easy. In fact most of the time it's hard getting so many people from different backgrounds and values to buy into each other. The carrot we continue to throw out to

*our team is that once we really allow ourselves to invest in
'our' TEAMWORK, we will become a very dangerous team.*

—JAY HOLMES
Texas A&M University Men's Head Coach

Through my commitment to TEAM, I was able to instill these beliefs to the assistant coaches, swimmers, and parents. All the pieces of TEAM play roles in very specific ways. Creating an atmosphere of commitment, trust, and caring within the team between swimmers and coaches led to individual and team success. There is no I in Team. TEAM takes many moving parts working together towards a common goal to be successful.

Chapter 3

THE CHAIR

The first week after I was hired at The Woodlands Swim Team they presented me with a chair. It was a folding director's chair embroidered with my name. It was a very nice chair that never saw a swim meet. How was I to expect results from the swimmers while they saw me sitting during their races? How do you coach from a chair? Put simply, you do not. I put a rule into effect that no Woodland's coach would sit when a team swimmer was in the water.

Before an upcoming meet I would consider which meet we were attending and which swimmers were going to the meet. I would then plan what events to place swimmers in to score maximum points, especially at all championship meets. Once at the meet swimmers were expected to wear proper team apparel, sit together, and support each other during all swim meets. Coaches also dressed appropriately. We also expected parents to wear team apparel and sit together so there was a sea of green in the stands to cheer on all the swimmers. Coaches were expected to engage with the swimmers and be available at all times. The swimmer would visit with their coach before each of their events as well as after their warm down following the race. These visits were quick in order to pump the swimmer up to do well or review the race. This was not the time to go over the race strategies in detail. I believe discussing strategies in detail right before a race leads to confusion for the swimmer. Over coaching before a race turns into overthinking and worry in the swimmer's mind. Most swimmers see their coach six days a week. The swimmer should be prepared for an upcoming meet having trained and prepared for their races during practices. At the meet all that should be required is a word of encouragement and maybe a few reminders. On meet day in many cases the more instruction a coach gives the swimmer the more likely to increase the chance of failure. What works for one swimmer may not work for another. Knowing your swimmer and what motivates them is key to successful swims.

Preparation before a swim meet is crucial for success. Knowledge about the layout of the pool takes the worry of the unknown out of the minds of swimmers. Knowing the events to be swum the day of the meet was the responsibility of the swimmer. If a swimmer has never been to a facility before, the internet is a great way to virtually tour the pool and layout. Everything from knowing what kind of starting block, size and color of the lane lanes, the look of the scoreboard and the depth of the pool all help swimmers prepare for an upcoming meet. For championship meets I would have them not only visualize their race but also the surroundings. I found visualization techniques to be one of the most beneficial ways to prepare for a meet. We started visualization techniques a week or two before the meet. I would instruct the swimmers to find a comfortable space that is quiet and dark. Bedtime is a great time to practice this technique.

First, focus on relaxing the body from head to toe relaxing each body part. Start relaxing the feet first then move your way up the body to the head while imagining that particular body part is heavy. Second, picture yourself in an elevator. With your eyes closed feel the elevator descend from the tenth floor to the first. Picture staring at the numbers counting down the floors on the wall of the elevator. Third, envision your favorite place, perhaps the beach or a park. As the elevator doors open see that place in front of you. Fourth, picture the pool you will be competing in; the entrance, stands full of parents, coaches and swimmers on the deck, the starting blocks, the lane lines, and the warm down pool. If you have not fallen asleep yet, picture going to the blocks for your first race. Finally, picture the feeling of excitement you feel before the race, then simply swim the race in your mind. Visualize the start, each stroke as you swim the length of the pool, the flip turns and you racing home to the finish line. Envisioning the entire race as well as the results on the scoreboard in your mind solidifies how you will swim your race physically in the pool. Training the mind is a huge factor for success, it gives you a distinct advantage over your competitors. If a swimmer has been coached properly, the race should come naturally at the meet.

A couple of years ago one of my teenage lesson swimmers called me on the way to her meet. When I asked her what events she was swimming that day, she had no idea. I could hear her ask her mother which told me she was not prepared for the meet. Parents are not the athlete. Younger age group swimmers will need more parent involvement. However in older swimmers knowing which events are being swam at meets is the swimmer's responsibility. Older swimmers should have this knowledge so they are prepared to race before ever getting to the pool. After this phone call, I worked with this swimmer on preparing for her races well before the next meet occurred. Several meets later I saw the swimmer and her mom at a meet. Mom asked me how her daughter should swim her race, I simply told my swimmer to go fast. I knew she was prepared this time. We had been preparing at practices leading up to the meet. She was prepared for success and dropped four seconds off her time in her best event. If a swimmer wants to be successful they need to take ownership of their races by preparing during practice and preparing their mind before meets. See it and Achieve it, be a swimmer 24/7.

Another aspect of coaching duties comes after a race has been swum. Reviewing the results are finding the good, the bad and the ugly. I did this much like a CEO of a business analyzes reports about the health of the company. After the meet was complete, I found time to review the results with the team. The only way to improve the team was to address opportunities head on and work on them with the swimmers. Each Monday following a meet we had a team meeting about what went well and what needed improving. We openly discussed the issues, and how we were going to fix the opportunities moving forward. We also had fun praising and celebrating the high points of the meet. This was the perfect catalyst going into the week. Following this formula seldom did mistakes occur twice. Remember the team is depending on you. Being active on the pool deck during meets allowed me to have more involvement with the whole team throughout the meet. I had the flexibility to meet with swimmers for warm ups or warm downs if needed, while also being available on the pool deck to watch races. I appreciated the chair the team gave me when I started coaching The Woodlands, but I would have never been able to be actively coaching the swimmers during the meet if I had sat in the chair the whole weekend.

Chapter 4

SEASON PLANNING

You cannot train all swimmers the same, just as you cannot taper all swimmers the same. The results would yield several successful swimmers, several failures, and overall a mediocre team. I see the swim season categorized into three phases: a beginning, middle, and end; all of which require different training. The following is a short breakdown of how I would plan a winter short course season. This is just an example of things to consider, most importantly though, your plan must match your team. A coach's plan must be unique based on the swimmer's and team's goals, not based on what another team or coach does.

September	Team meetings, goal setting, select team captains, introduce drylands, stroke work, begin aerobic training, adjust groups by age and ability
October	Increase aerobic training, continue team meetings, stroke work, and dryland training. Introduce weight training (if available), start distance lane twice a week
November	Aerobic training adjusted to individuals, group levels starting to take shape, introduce sprint and breaststroke lanes, adjust weight training to specified groups
December	Keep specific groups but increase yardage and intensity. If you have a champ meet to make cuts for year-end meets keep yardage up but decrease intensity and stay off weights week of meet.

January	Distance lanes increase yardage with hard intervals three times a week, sprint lanes increase intensity with recovery three times a week.
February/ March	Pretaper and taper begins depending on when the meet will occur, which group, events the swimmer is swimming, and how many meets the swimmer is participating in, which is discussed in the next chapter.

September was the month to focus on setting team dynamics and lay out expectations for the season. We held short team meetings before practice concentrating on individual and team goals and placing swimmers in groups by ability.

A quick side note. I feel I should address taper at the beginning of the season because a common question all coaches get from swimmers is "when does a taper start?" I explain my answer to them early in the season that a taper starts the first day of the season when a swimmer shows up to the first practice. I emphasize each practice is important and will affect end season results. Attendance and work ethic together are what makes a taper possible. This becomes the swimmer's commitment to excellence.

One important responsibility a coach has is by placing swimmers in the proper training groups. Two things to consider are the age and ability of the swimmer. In my consideration I always broke it down to five percent age (to keep parents happy) and ninety five percent ability level. The main factor I considered when placing swimmers into groups was ability level. I rarely looked at age as an element of placing swimmers. Placing swimmers by age alone will limit the swimmer to the ability of that particular group. This group may not be the same ability level which in turn places a cap to the intensity of workouts for fast swimmers. I have placed twelve-year-olds on the national team and achieved great success. When a swimmer is talented, placing them in a more advanced group will push the swimmer to excel to a higher level where the workouts, intervals, and expectations are much higher. Swimmers almost always rise to those expectations and have success. The age and maturity level of the swimmer are less to be concerned with. Some parents resist allowing their kids to swim in higher level groups because of fears the older athletes may influence the younger ones. I have found that to be mostly untrue. When swimming at this higher level, the swimmer's commitment to the pool is the priority; it is not a social hour.

Once swim groups are established the real training begins with each month building off the previous month's training. After beginning stroke work and aerobic conditioning we added drylands and plyometrics.

DRYLANDS

A dryland program can be implemented for all ages. An athlete's core and ab muscles were my number one focus. Those muscle groups affect all four strokes and play a major role in training. In older groups, completing your program with body weight strength exercises rounds out this portion of your dryland program. Drylands should be administered by groups and when one or two team members cannot or do not complete the drill, the entire group has to repeat together until all can do that particular exercise in the given time. Now you are bringing Team into dryland training. The athletes will encourage and cheer each other on in order to complete the exercises. I felt it important to challenge the team to work together, depend, and encourage each other in as well as outside of the pool.

PLYOMETRICS

I define plyometrics as any type of jumping exercise, some examples are wall jumping, jumping rope, and box jumping. All play a part in the swimmer's fitness level by including specific jumps for specific groups. Sprinters should spend the most time training the white twitch muscle fiber as they train to increase their vertical jump ability and their reaction skill off the start. This also improves the swimmer's bounce off the wall, as opposed to flip, plant, and push. The word bounce is key to sprint turns. An original idea to emphasize the bounce technique is to place a small trampoline in the pool vertically covering the turning cross. This now causes the swimmers to truly bounce off the turns. Before long you will notice a change at the other end of the pool during turns with bouncing off the walls with no trampoline involved. Applying the word bounce to turns does make a difference no matter the length or stroke of the event.

Plyometrics will enhance your events for middle and distance endurance as well. Springing off the blocks and bouncing off the wall during turns are little details which make a big impact in total time dropped during any length race. By practicing these during every workout they become part of the swimmer's muscle memory and not something to think about before a race. To make plyometrics fun each season we had a jump rope contest to see who could do the most jumps in three minutes. This was a fun team building event in which all team members participated.

WEIGHTS

Importantly, take age group swimmers out of the equation for weight lifting. Damage can occur to parts of the body that are still growing if an adolescent age group swimmer lifts weights. However, body strength exercises such as pull ups, dips, and push-ups are excellent choices until they reach the age in which weight lifting is appropriate. Once a swimmer is no longer an adolescent and weights are introduced, specific care and proper technique must be emphasized to avoid injury.

Also, I believe just like training in the water, weights should be individualized based on events swum. At The Woodlands, we divided the swimmers into three different weight programs for sprinters, middle distance, and distance swimmers. The sprinters would lift weights three times a week doing a three round circuit adding weight each round for approximately one hour. The middle distance would lift twice a week using slightly less weight but doing several repetitions at each station for approximately forty-five minutes. The distance swimmers would lift one or two times per week using very little weight. When possible their stroke count would dictate the amount of repetitions per minute of lifting.

For age group swimmers emphasis should be placed on building technique of all four strokes at all distances. This gives younger swimmers the opportunity to hone skills and explore which type of events they are best suited to swim. The senior level swimmers should have more diversity in training than age group swimmers to be successful. For both groups having each practice build on the next in intensity was important going into October and the middle of the season when workout intensity increases. Our meetings in October would be used for preparation for upcoming meets. On land as well as in the pool I split swimmers into different groups based on the events and distances they swam in order to individualize workouts. This allowed training for individual strokes, sprints, and distance swimming separately. First I took into consideration sprint or distance, then built in specific days for stroke work.

Once sprint and distant lanes were established, practices would then get more specified. Specialized training began two days a week to begin with in September and three days by mid-November. The sprint lane emphasis was on anaerobic sets with recovery. The sprinters will begin to take pride in themselves and their accomplishments in practice. As a coach it is important to notice where a swimmer is weak and seek out new methods to improve those opportunities. Or perhaps it is looking for alternative ways to combat bad habits. On a side note, trying different things can be beneficial. At one point I had noticed one of my sprinters, Adam had a great down kick but was weak on his up kick. I brought a cinder block wrapped in a towel to practice and had him hold the block on his chest while kicking sprint twenty-fives on his back. By the end of the season he qualified for finals at the U.S. Olympic Trials in the fifty meter freestyle. This swimmer's determination and hard work reminds me of the title of Sam Freas' book "Sprinting, It Takes Guts" and how that is such a true statement. I have learned coaching the fifty yard freestyle is much harder than coaching the sixteen hundred fifty yard freestyle.

Like the sprint lanes, I started the distance lanes with two days a week and moved to three days as the swimmers began to handle the increased yardage. My primary focus was aerobic training and pace work. I did not limit the distance to freestyle, I mixed in four hundred yard individual medley type sets to offer a variety in training. Once again pride will be established within the group as they achieve their accomplishments. An example of a typical set for the distance lane would have equaled about 6,000 yards:

1 x 800 freestyle @ 12:00 minutes with 1:30 holding intervals

1 x 400 IM @ 6:00 minutes

1 x 800 freestyle @ 11:20 minutes with 1:25 holding intervals

1 x 400 IM @ 5:45 minutes

1 x 800 freestyle @ 10:40 minutes with 1:20 holding intervals

1 x 400 IM @ 5:30 minutes

1 x 800 freestyle @ 10:00 minutes with 1:15 holding intervals

1 x 400 IM @ 5:15 minutes

1 x 800 freestyle @ 9:20 minutes

1x 400 IM @ 5:00 minutes

Now here is where I would get creative: on each 400 IM I had the swimmer add an extra breaststroke pull out on the third turn.

During the 800 freestyles on the last 100 you get x amount of breaths. Now all of sudden coaching the distance lane was not so boring.

The breaststroke lane, all teams need one, twice a week for most. Breaststroke being the one stroke that does not complement the others will need special attention for both individual medley and breaststroke swimmers. I designated a coach that could commit to these swimmers. They need different intervals, while also incorporating various and specific drills to be the best they can be. I believe if one wants to swim the individual medley then one must embrace breaststroke. It is not just twenty five percent of the race, the time spent in the water compared to the other strokes is different. We can use an average high school male's 200 yard individual medley time splits: Butterfly 27:00 seconds, Backstroke 30:00 seconds, Breastroke36:00 seconds, Freestyle 27:00 seconds. As one can see the breaststroke leg is nine seconds longer than the butterfly or freestyle legs, now double those splits for the 400 individual medley. It is to the swimmer's advantage to take care in paying special attention to breaststroke training.

Middle distance as well as individual stroke swimmers work well together. Like breaststroke we had designated lanes for backstroke, butterfly, and freestyle. Now that all strokes and distances have been addressed the final pieces of the puzzle will fit together. With many moving parts swimmers come together as a team while training their individual skill set. This is similar to how the military or a football team train individuals in their specialized positions to lead the team to total success. Wow, now you have a recipe to start winning as a team. As the final phase of the season approaches in February it is time to start considering rests and tapers. This is the scariest part of the season for any coach. Done right the swimmer will have great success, but done wrong the swimmer will not achieve the best he or she can be.

Chapter 5

TAPER

What is a taper? What is the difference between rest and taper? Why does it work or not work? When does it start? How long does it last? Age group versus senior, male versus female, sprinter versus distance swimmer are just a few things to consider when beginning to taper. I told you taper was a scary subject and I will answer all of the above and more. First I need to preface this with a warning, tapering age group swimmers is an entirely different process which I address later in the chapter.

Let me address resting first. Resting is a short term process done by keeping yardage up but lessening intensity a week or so before a meet. This process allows the swimmer a small amount of recovery time in order to gain energy for one meet. Then you can pick intensity back up and continue training without losing a step. I like to describe it as a nap during the day when you are tired. Naps give a person a short amount of energy in order to get to the end of the day for a full night's sleep. I equate taper to jumping off a cliff. Amount of yardage is not as important as what the swimmer does with the yardage they are swimming. Yardage will usually drop significantly dependent on the type of swimmer. Taper is a longer process similar to resting, but done over a longer period of time. A taper includes resting and can be incorporated into a couple of meets. Also during a taper the type of swimmer should be considered. Tapering a sprinter is different from tapering a distance swimmer.

Eddie Reese once stated in a clinic that taper probably started when some team all got sick enough to miss several practices before a meet. During the meet the swimmers swam fast. Taper to me is a time to allow the body to recover and rest before a big competition. Depending on the training the swimmer completed over the course of the season, this will dictate their specific taper; drylands, weights, even lifestyle away from the practice arena play a role.

My worst taper. This is a story that depicts failure, yet is a great example to help coaches, swimmers, and parents understand the delicate balance of tapering. Early on at my time at The Woodlands, the team had five female swimmers qualify for Junior National in Northern California. I was excited as we flew out a couple of days early. The first evening we were there I bought the swimmers a steak dinner. The following day we did not go to the pool, but instead I took them to Fisherman's Wharf in San Francisco. We walked for hours and had so much fun. The best swim of the five day meet came from a swimmer who added seven seconds to her 200 butterfly. At first I blamed the swimmers, but after thinking about the week I realized I was to blame for the failure. I was not being a swim coach but a tour guide instead. Two years later we won our first Junior National Team Championship. After that meet, I always said as a swim coach you have to realize you are not their mom, dad, or friend. Swimmers will respect you, the coach, and great results will follow.

Dick Jochums once answered a great question at an ASCA (American Swim Coaches Association) clinic. What do you do if the swimmer does everything you ask while never missing a practice and fails? Dick's response was the best answer possible: One, you do not blame the swimmer, you take account it was your fault. Two, you tell the swimmer what you, the coach, will do to fix it next season. Three, you hope they are not a senior in high school. By being honest and taking responsibility you will not lose that swimmer's trust. From experience in San Francisco I made some changes to how I approach the team experience during away meets.

We no longer went sight-seeing at the locations where swim meets occurred. We stayed off our feet whenever possible, remember the Fisherman's Wharf story? Outside pool activities can ruin a good taper, rest your legs. We would have team meetings at the hotel, not the pool. Perhaps one of the biggest changes occurred around meal time. Whenever possible we ate breakfast together, and I also had dinners brought to the hotel so we could eat together as a team.

TAPERING DISTANCE SWIMMERS

A general fact of tapering distance swimmers should be that yardage does not go down, especially with girls, practice intensity gets tapered to a point for that individual. For example, a former female swimmer, Lori Walker, was trained with a great deal of yardage. Somewhere in the range of 10,000 to 20,000 yards depending on the time of year with recovery days in between. During tapering intensity (pace, heart rate, stroke rate) of practices decreased and yardage dropped to approximately 6,000 yards. When we arrived at a Senior Nationals in North Carolina her yardage was kept at 6,000 yards. The day of the 500 yard freestyle we woke up early and went to the pool to do a 3,000 yard wake up swim. Afterwards we met the rest of the team for breakfast before going back to the pool to get in another 3,000 yard swim. For a warm up swim before her race she swam about 400 yards with a couple of pace fifties. She swam a 4:47 and placed second to the world record holder, Janet Evans. Lori taught me a valuable lesson that season which helped many future distance swimmers go fast. A long distance swimmer who trains with high yardage in practice during the season does not need to significantly decrease yardage during taper in order to go fast.

SPRINT TAPERING

The most important part of training a sprinter during the peak of the season was intensity of the workout not the amount of yardage.

For most sprinters at the peak of training the yardage could have been in the 5,000–7,000 range. When it came to tapering we stepped off a cliff and dropped off the yardage significantly. I never really believed in a stair step taper, especially for sprinters. For sprinters it is not about the amount you swim but what you are doing with the yards they are swimming. The idea is to keep the muscle fibers firing, but also have recovery time. Most swimmers will have what is known as a dead zone, the dog days approximately seven to ten days away from the meet, especially sprinters, may appear to be getting slower. Their body is adapting to rest, it is a terrible and scary time for both swimmer and coach. A typical coach's response may be to add yardage, but in reality the opposite is true. Both need to believe in themselves and the taper process. I once had a senior 100 butterflyer trying to break the fifty second mark. I had him swim a broken one hundred at top speed one week out from Senior Nationals; his time was 51.8 seconds. Obviously I was scared to death wondering what I did wrong. I told him that was a perfect time for a week out. I also increased his rest believing in the taper process. One week later at Senior Nationals he swam a 48.6. Here again a swimmer coaches the coach. You need to believe and have faith in the taper process. Senior sprinters are a special breed, get to know them, trust them and they will trust you. Knowing your swimmers, do not be afraid to rest. Rule of thumb: males need more rest than females, the number of events to be swum makes a difference, weights and drylands also need to be tapered. Rest is rest in every aspect of training. Once swimmers believe in the taper process great results will happen. "When in doubt, get out" (Eddie Reese).

SUITS AND SHAVING DOWN

First of all I believe speed suits should only be worn for championship meets. Unfortunately I see too many swimmers wearing elite suits for regular swim meets. Speed suits give the swimmer a slickness feel through the water. When a swimmer wears a speed suit all the time there will be no difference for the feel in the water during championship meets. As for shaving, the purpose is to open the pores of the skin causing the water to bead up and fall away. Water will cling to hair causing drag, but when a swimmer shaves this too gives a slickness feel in the water. Shaving and speed suits are for championship meets only. If a swimmer expects a taper to work, then the swimmer needs to swim fast unshaven while wearing a team suit, not the $500 champ suits now available.

BREASTSTROKE AND OTHER TAPERS

I felt it necessary to separate breaststroke swimmers because they are special. There are two groups of breaststrokers, the classic 50/100 yard breaststroke swimmer who may get up to 200 yard distance or the 200/400 breaststroke/individual medley swimmer, seldom are they the same. I believe training the classic breaststroke swimmer should fall into a separate category during both training and taper. The true 400 individual medley swimmer or 200 breaststroke swimmer fall into a different group, here again separation is key.

I cannot taper swimmers who I have not worked with because tapering is an individual process. The most important piece of tapering is knowing your swimmers. It does not matter if they are butterflyers, backstrokers, or middle distance freestylers; 100 or 200 yard swimmers or both, they need to be tapered as individuals as much as possible. Male or female, workload, weights, and size all play a part in the swimmers success and the team success. Coaches, swimmers, as well as parents can support each other. I always believe the team must come first. No one athlete on the team is more important than anyone else. Those that believe the other will never achieve team success. "There is no I in team" this includes swimmers, coaches, and parents. When we can come together as a team and embrace "Oneness" we can achieve great things.

John on the pool deck having a relay meeting before a race.

AGE GROUP TAPERING

Someone once said "put a fast suit on them and tell them they are tapered." Okay, not that easy. Most age group swimmers have boundless energy anytime of day. They have not reached the age where muscles need recovery. Controlling the energy level and letting it build up until meet day is the key for younger swimmers. Examples of controlling energy would be to walk not run, sit not walk, sleep not sit. The basics to consider are one, keep yardage up, my rule was to not go under 5,000 yards per day. Two, maturity level and body development does play a part. And three, it is fine to cut intensity per day as the champ meet approaches. By cutting yardage too much, an age group swimmer will lose the feel for the water and their confidence will go down. By keeping yardage up and decreasing intensity the swimmer will keep the feel of the water and will perform better at the big meet. Age group swimmers are an integral part of a winning team; they should not be babied. Remember the team comes first and they are part of the team. When they feel important to the team goal and know they will be held accountable, age group swimmers will swim fast; not just for themselves but for the team. United States Swimming is a sport that builds swimmers to the highest level they can be, it is not for anyone who wants something for nothing. To win, coaches, parents, and swimmers must support each other to be the best they can be through dedication and high expectations for everyone. The following is an interesting fact: at The Woodlands Swim Team we won our first age group state championship with only one hundred and twenty-four total swimmers on the team. However, we qualified seventy six of those swimmers for our age group state championship (TAGS). This number is over fifty percent of the swimmers on the team qualifying for the meet. The success lies in everyone believing in Team.

John Vogel had a way of making his swimmers believe they could achieve goals and times that sometimes seemed completely out of reach. He emphasized "no I in Team" and spent time with each swimmer setting individual goals that would ultimately contribute towards the team goals. I came to swim for TWST in the summer of 1983. I lived in Lake Jackson, about 85 miles south of the Woodlands, and there were plenty of closer teams but decided this was the best program for me, and we were willing to make the commitment. The team goal that summer was to win the long course TAGS, to bring home the Texas state championship banner for the first time for this team. John also helped me set a personal goal of winning five individual events at TAGS...not something I would have come up with for myself, but one that John believed I could do. I remember thinking at the time it seemed impossible, but agreed to work towards that. As a secondary "goal," I made a bet with my dad that if I won five events, he would quit smoking. He had smoked for over twenty years but decided to accept my challenge, later admitting that he thought it was a nice goal to have but not likely to happen. We all trained harder than we ever had that summer, and our team goal of winning TAGS was accomplished, as well as my personal goals, including getting my dad to quit smoking…great accomplishments all around! It was a summer to remember…team commitments that would extend long after the summer and the beginning of life-long friendships.

—KRISTI KIGGINS BARTELSMAN
Former TWST swimmer

*Flag from the first TAGS Championship win for
The Woodlands Swim Team.*

John Vogel

Chapter 6

HIGH SCHOOL…THE UNLIKELY, THE IMPOSSIBLE

Somehow towards the end of my coaching career at The Woodlands I was talked into coaching the local high school swim team by the Athletic Director. The previous coach quit during the summer, and I suppose I was a natural choice. At the time I was Head Coach of The Woodlands Swim Team and Head Aquatic Director at The Woodlands Athletic Center. We had swimmers from over seven different high school teams on The Woodlands Swim Team. I was familiar with the swimmers on this high school team.

Once I agreed to take on the task; I called a team meeting for my new high school team. I told them our goal should be to win the Texas High School State Championship. They quickly informed me "we can't win." Evidently the team who won the state championship the year before won by seventy six points and had not one student graduate. Our high school team finished third and lost a forty-eight second 100 yard flyer as well as two great sprint freestylers. To win the state championship seemed to be conquering the impossible. After listening to how great our competition was for far too long, our meeting got real. I do not believe in the impossible, and after that meeting in September neither did our team. They were not allowed to leave the meeting until each team member said something positive about our team. I wanted to shift the team's mentality into appreciating all they had to offer and see the talent sitting in the very room. Some comments I heard that day were "well we have a freshman backstroker that might win," "we have a lot of depth and might get three relays to the meet." These were definitely positive aspects of the team. After I listened to them talk for a bit, they started to believe they could win. By looking at only their strengths, they quickly forgot about the other team. They talked themselves into believing they could win. The desire to achieve the goal was solidified within the team and the swimmers began to push and support each other. Jack Nelson, long time Ft. Lauderdale coach and 1976 US Olympic Team coach once said "Believe to Achieve."

The second thing I did as a new high school coach was schedule a dual meet with this "unbeatable" team. The stands were filled with parents, students and both the Athletic Director and Principal were in attendance. We were ready, or so I thought. The coach of this state championship team decided to bring his junior varsity swimmers instead of the varsity team. Normally I would never run the score up on a team, we would score enough to win but not over dominate the other team. However, in this case I told the score table to score every point...Game On! My intention was to have our team see the opportunity was there to beat the state champions. By winning the dual meet, the team gained more confidence that the goal of winning the state championship was within reach. We went undefeated that season and also won our district and regional meets. Next meet was the State Championship. The state meet could not have gone better. It was one of the best meets I have ever coached. Our swimmers Believed and performed above and beyond all expectations. Everything discussed back in that September meeting plus more happened. "Believe to Achieve" actually happened that day in Austin, Texas. This reminded me of what Coach Bussard, my college swimming coach, used to say "winning is living." After the meet, we went out for a steak dinner to celebrate. As I arrived at the restaurant, one of the parents met me with a big hug. He was so excited the team had won the State Championship.

Swim TEAM?

Football. Played it. Loved it. Followed it. The ultimate team sport. Swimming was what we did in a pond or lake to cool off in the summer. But in 1989 I was transferred to Houston and settled in The Woodlands. That is where my sons and family were first introduced to TWST and the SPORT of swimming. That is where we met Coach John Vogel. It was our introduction into the "Team is Family" culture fostered by John and his staff of dedicated coaches.

*Being a consistent winner, in any sport and at any level, is rare. But it does happen. Winning can become contagious. Coach Vogel guided TWST to its first TAGS title in 1983.By the end of his tenure, TWST had won 26 TAGS titles, and eight Junior National swim titles. For many years TWST was the team to beat in the Gulf, Texas and the USA.***WHY?TEAM.** *And it worked like this. The team makes the individual better, and the individual makes the team better. In practice and competition, each swimmer was challenged to give his or her best. During meets every swimmer's goal was to swim best times and score points for the* **TEAM***. That attitude permeated every age group level, the coaching staff and the parent teams that organized and worked all meets at the Woodlands Athletic Center. These individual strands wound together to form a strong rope, and each strand was recognized as being an integral part of the* **TEAM***'s success. Top to bottom: bottom to top.* **TEAM.** *Everybody bought in. While parents supported their own kids, each kid was supported and encouraged because they all were "our TWST kids."*

One of John's biggest challenges came in 1995.The Woodlands McCullough head swim coach had resigned just before the beginning of the school year. John was offered the job for one year, the 1995–96 swim season. He accepted and immediately went to work. Fortunately much of his team was made up of TWST swimmers, so John was very familiar with their capabilities. After swimming their way through the season and the district and regional meets, McCullough qualified a strong team for the UIL State meet in the Texas Swim Center, Austin. That team would face the defending state champs, Cypress Creek. Creek was the team to beat, though on paper that seemed unlikely, But as John often said, "the meet is swum in the POOL, not on paper!" And he was RIGHT!

—BILL RADFORD
Team Parent & Grill Master
1989–1998

Boy's team on the podium accepting the winning trophy at the Texas State High School Championship meet.

Texas State Championship flag

Chapter 7

DONUTS

read an article this summer about committing to excellence, in which several Olympic coaches contributed to the article. One concept that stood out was the athlete's commitment to excellence both in and out of the water. Certainly hard work in the water was a focus, but we all believe in that; however, life outside the pool plays a pivotal role for the elite athlete as well. Elite athletes go beyond committing in the pool. They change their lifestyle by committing to excellence twenty four hours a day. Proper sleep, outside activities, and diet play a role in the athlete's desire to commit to excellence. Lifestyle either contributes or takes away from a swimmer's performance while training or while attending meets.

The amount of sleep each night is important, the body needs eight to ten hours to properly reset every night. Elite athletes might choose to sleep while sacrificing other interests in order to achieve the needed rest to be able to train at peak performance. A question to consider for the elite athlete is "do outside activities or habits during the day impact my ability to train hard during workouts?

What you eat as well as what you do not eat or drink play a huge role in committing to excellence. Eddie Reese once suggested in a coaches clinic to have your swimmers look at their plate at each meal before eating and ask themselves "is this going to make me swim faster?" I encourage all my swimmers to make healthy food choices. I compare it to driving my old 1969 Corvette. If I had put low quality gas in the tank, the car would have run horribly. By putting high quality gas in the tank, my Corvette ran better and extended the life of the car. Swimmers should see their bodies like it is that Corvette, a top performing sports car. What you put in your body is what you get out of your body. Snacks are needed for proper nutritional balance as long they are helping the body train or recover from training. With the internet this information is readily available.

Now you may be wondering what about those donuts? To illustrate this point about nutrition to the team at The Woodlands each season I asked the team to not eat donuts during the course of the season. I was bringing team, sacrifice, and proper nutrition together with this simple request. The entire coaching staff and I were to follow the same commitment with the team as well. This was an entire team affair. One day after practice I was driving home and noticed a fender bender on the side of the road involving a couple of my senior swimmers. I pulled over to help them. After making sure everyone was alright, I walked into a local establishment to call the girls' parents. Yes, this was before we had a phone in our pocket. When I came out I had not even realized I had been in a donut shop. Later that season at our banquet, the girls out of fun presented a picture of me leaving that shop. To this day I have never touched a donut. I have done this as a mental reminder to myself of all the sacrifice I ask my swimmers to make each year. Years later I was at a pool when I witnessed a couple of parents and coaches passing out donuts one week before the state meet. Sure it may have been fun in the moment; however, were those parents, coaches, and athletes considering how those donuts affect performance? Unfortunately for the swimmers they did not. Commitment to excellence not only comes from the athlete, but should be inspired and led by parents and the coaching staff. Commitment to being an elite athlete is twenty four hours a day to be the best you can be.

John in front of the infamous donut shop.

PARTICIPATION OR COMMITTING TO EXCELLENCE

I have seen a recent trend with some teams who believe the number of swimmers on a team will lead to more success, the thought being more swimmers equals more winning. However, this is not always true. Commitment to achieve excellence and a winning team starts at the top with coaches and trickles down to the swimmers. If the coach has the belief that the team can win and leads by example to set the winning formula, the swimmers will follow the winning attitude. There will be swimmers on a team who are not the fastest in the pool, but they are committed to always showing up to be the best they can be in the pool. These athletes are just as important as the fastest swimmers on the team, sometimes they will surprise themselves or the coach and end up in a points position. These athletes are committed to support the team and are part of TEAM. TEAM is not just participation, it is commitment to excellence whatever the speed may be. When a coach is dedicated to TEAM, these athletes will not be ignored and will be celebrated for the commitment it takes to be part of TEAM.

On the other hand, you have the swimmer who shows up and takes up space. I know this sounds cruel, but this is reality. These swimmers are just participating by showing up and swimming in a lane. They are not striving to be the best they can be. These swimmers do not have individual goals or commit to excellence. The attitude they have is get in the pool then get out. These swimmers do not support TEAM concepts. I see this behavior in age group swimmers often. They may be there because their parents are making them "do something." Or perhaps the cause could be that this current age group of children expect something for nothing. This is the reason I do not believe in participation ribbons. Participation ribbons given for just showing up will water down the desire to work hard. The desire to work harder is no longer needed to achieve individual or team success.

When The Woodlands Swim Team was inducted into the Texas Swimming Hall of Fame in 2019 I spoke at the banquet, I was asked "tell us about having fun." My answer: Having fun in swimming is winning, fun is being the underdog and touching the wall first, fun is being on the podium, fun is throwing the coach in the pool after winning a meet, fun is the energy from swimming your best, most of all fun is being the best you can be.

In the early 1980's the team was attending the Junior National Meet in Milwaukee, Wisconsin. Three boys in attendance broke one of the major team rules. Earlier in my career I would have thrown them off the team, but decided to try something different this time. I had the boys meet me at the pool at 6:00 am the day after returning from the meet. I explained they were off the team and why, but gave each one a chance to earn a place back on the team. I also told them it would be a difficult experience. I did not expect the boys to agree, but they did. We would meet at the running track every day after practice for a week. If they did everything at the track they could stay on the team. The first day I set time goals for various lengths of running which had to be met or they would start over. The first boy said he could not do it because of a knee problem, so I told him he was off the team. Next the second boy could not make the time intervals the second day, so he was off the team. However the third boy could run.

He came every day to every workout and accomplished every interval. On the fifth and final day he had to run ten 440's under seventy seconds each. It was raining and he was wearing full warmups. If he missed an interval he had to start over. I could not believe this kid had been doing all the running and intervals. I really wanted to make an example and not let him back on the team for breaking this rule. On the ninth 440, I walked out to the track and tripped him up. I thought he would quit. I told him he missed the interval and he had to start over. The boy looked at me and said "Yes Sir" and started over. He ran ten more 440's and at the end I hugged him. This boy was committed to swimming and the team. He made a mistake, but more than paid his dues. Before this week had occurred he had not told his parents what had happened on the trip. After he left the track that day he told his parents what he had done. This swimmer grew up to be one of my best friends. I learned a lot from him that week. Most importantly, if a person is willing to take responsibility for his actions, he is worth keeping. Never give up on athletes with this quality. After he was a grown adult he still came to TAGS to support the team and play our team music at the beginning of our meets.

Once a team environment is created it must be maintained and nurtured daily. While preparing to write this book, I studied several elite coaches and their teams. Each of these coaches have coached at the Olympic level. Eddie Reese from the University of Texas, Jack Bauerle from University of Georgia, and Mark Schubert from Mission Viejo all have created a strong team atmosphere not only at the team level, but the U.S. Olympic Team level as well. I have had the privilege to know Jack Bauerle since the early 1990's. Here is something written by Coach Bauerle about building a great team.

> *Perhaps the most important part of making a good team great is making sure of roles and having the athletes realize that each one of them matters and they do! If you have good leaders, let them lead. Two of my greatest NCAA championship teams, I literally had three meetings the entire year. To be able to leave it in the hands of your seniors when you know your staff and you have done a good job. The fastest swimmers have a big responsibility other than just swimming fast they need to be great teammates. When swimmers swim for others rather than just themselves, you have the makings of a good team A&E. Attitude and Effort will take you to the promised land. We promote a willingness to swim any event that helps the team which gets 'extra' points that are needed to win. Here's an aside: in an eighteen year stretch we were National Champions or runner up twenty-five out of eighteen years without a home loss. The culture was a winning one but that was presided over with understanding that being a great teammate and being willing to sacrifice for the team was paramount and that to toughness every day.*

> —JACK BAUERLY
> Head Swim Coach at the University of Georgia

What starts out with something as simple as giving up a donut can snowball into a swimmer becoming a twenty-four hour a day elite swimmer. It is a reminder of the lifestyle elite athletes follow on a daily basis to perform at their absolute best. Once, while I was speaking at a TISCA clinic I asked the group of coaches how many people had bacon and eggs for breakfast. Many coaches raised their hands. I then explained that the chicken had participated in the breakfast by providing the eggs, but the pig committed to the breakfast by providing the bacon. Committing to excellence is a full time commitment that not only includes training but lifestyle as well. I always ask my swimmers to ask themselves this question, "Will this help me be the best swimmer I can be?"

Caption reads: Best of the Best. Woodlands coaches John Vogel (left) and Joel Engel celebrated a ninth-straight GULF swimming championship with TWST high-point winners (from left) Sean Galegher, Suzanne Steres, T.J. Fry, Lisa Rhodes and Jeff Thibault

Chapter 8

TEAM CAPTAINS

A Coach's Lifeline

Team captains as well as the senior level group will play a valuable role in maintaining a team atmosphere. The captains represented the swimmers on the whole team, led team meetings, and were cheerleaders for the team. It was important to choose a senior level swimmer as a captain because of maturity level, experience, and leadership skills. At the beginning of the season every swimmer cast a vote for captains. I devised a point system based on swim level. The younger swim level votes counted as one point then the point values went up from there with each level. The senior level points carried more weight because these were the peers that knew the potential captains. Team captains were my lifeline to what was going on with the swimmers from their perspective. We would meet regularly and discuss any issues or concerns. If something did come up, I gave the captains the option of handling the situation themselves or have me step in to help. Most times the captain could resolve the situation without help from myself.

A second task team captains did was lead team meetings. Through team meetings they instilled confidence in the younger swimmers. The captains would inspire their peers through hard work, positive attitudes, and perseverance. They led by example which really helped solidify the bonds created within the team. Another role they served was as coaches at our annual green and white intersquad meet. We divided the team into two, a green team and a white team of which the team captains were coach for each one of those teams. Those intersquad meets were some of the most fun meets we swam. Once drafted to a team that swimmer would remain with their green or white team as long as they were on the swim team, led by the team captains.

1997 Team Captain Hollie Childress

One season early on in my career I think we set a record for first alternates (ninth place finishes) at the state championship. I was having a hard time getting the kids to swim fast in prelims every time in order to qualify for finals. The very next season I found a meet one month before the Texas state meet in Bartlesville, Oklahoma. Before going to the meet I had a meeting with my team captains to devise a plan to get the younger swimmers committed to swimming fast in prelims. What we came up with was genius, if the age group swimmers were not swimming well, I would give a signal for the team captains to take over. The Bartlesville pool was a small six lane pool, and once again we were not performing well in prelims. Frustrated with the team and myself, I told the captains to take over coaching duties and walked off the pool deck. This caught the younger swimmers attention that, or the captains were better coaches than me on that day. As soon as the captains took over they inspired the younger swimmers to swim faster. They pumped the swimmers up and cheered them on. We were outstanding in the prelims the following two mornings. We not only won that meet, but a month later we won the state championship with no first alternates.

The team began to learn the importance of swimming fast during prelims. This later proved to be the winning ingredient to winning Junior Nationals, swim fast in prelims became the rule. The following two years we returned to the same Bartlesville meet to reinforce the importance of prelim swims. Learning to be fast in morning swims was a huge part of our Junior National, Senior National, and Olympic Trial success.

Team captains were the biggest cheerleaders for the other swimmers at meets. They supported those swimmers in and out of the pool. I cannot praise the team captains enough of which I had the privilege of coaching at The Woodlands. At another TAGS meet we had a ten and under swimming in the first event in finals. This swimmer had to leave our team meeting early to get to the blocks on time. This swimmer was in lane eight, so the captains came up with a plan to line the pool deck to support her for the race. After the meeting we walked out as a team and lined the pool deck to cheer her on. The energy the team showed was amazing, and this swimmer pulled out the win for ten and under fifty backstroke from lane eight!

Everyone has had the feeling of intimidation for some reason or another in life. Maybe it was lack of confidence over a test at school or trying something new for the first time. One of the main functions of a head coach is inspiring confidence in each swimmer by teaching them how to cast aside those negative thoughts. Using the experience the captains brought to the team we were able to lessen those fears in order to be successful. When younger swimmers see the older swimmers have confidence they will learn how to handle themselves at meets. Learning to not fear the competition is such an important aspect of swimming, and knowing that believing is achieving. Swim with confidence and success will follow. Believing in yourself and your team is a key ingredient to a swimmer's success. At the University of Tennessee our conference championship ring had four letters on them, ~~AAAO~~. It was more an attitude than a word…we will swim Anyone, Anytime, Anyplace Bar Nothing. I instilled this belief in my swimmers to never be afraid to swim anyone.

John's class ring from the University of Tennessee

At our age group state championship meet a dear friend as well as ex-swimmer was in charge of the music we walked out to at finals.

As soon as the national anthem ended, our music started and outwalked The Woodlands Swim Team. Intimidating...you bet. Imagine seventy plus swimmers led by the team captains, dressed the same, walking out to the song Eye of the Tiger. We were ready to race, depending on each other, supporting each other as one, "Oneness." We were Team.

Team captains played an integral part in the success we had at The Woodlands. They helped pick out team shirts, organized team events, served as the swimmer's voice to the coach, represented the team at functions, and spoke at team meetings. Teams need the leadership from their peers to set the example for success. Team captains will inspire everyone to work together and embrace TEAM. It was such a privilege to work with outstanding swimmers and instill great leadership qualities to them. Coaching and getting to know these leaders made me a better coach.

The Woodlands Swim Team picture from 1984

Chapter 9

JUNIOR NATIONALS
AND BEYOND

Once we learned to prepare for fast prelim swimming, it was time to step up for success at the national level. We had been winning TAGS for years. There had to be a mental shift in the team for performing at the national level to achieve the same level of success we had at the state level. The main difference was fewer swimmers at the meet which means the individual swims became more essential. Every swim was important. Swimming fast in prelims was key to propel the swimmers into the final heats. In order to win meets at the national level the expectation had to be that if you qualified for a meet you were expected to score. Instead of just qualifying for Junior Nationals, we were scoring points. To motivate the swimmers to push themselves, I made a box and painted it black. I told the whole team the recipe to winning on a national level was in the box. What made this black box so special was only the swimmers who had qualified for Junior Nationals or above could look in the box. The curiosity surrounding the black box and what it held was motivation enough. Swimmers could not wait to see what was in the black box. When a swimmer made the qualifying cut they would come to my office to look inside. What did they find? As they opened the box they found a mirror angled to where they could only see themselves. I told them the recipe for winning and being successful was themselves. Amazingly no one ever mentioned what was in the box, it was a secret not to be shared.

The first Junior National meet we won was in Long Beach, California. Coincidentally, this is where the University of Tennessee won their national championship. Looking at the heat sheet our highest seeded swimmer on day one of the meet was Lindsey Etter in the 200 breaststroke seeded twenty sixth. With a fast prelim swim she qualified for finals and placed second, and we found ourselves after day one winning the meet. With that swim as starting inspiration the rest of the team followed swimming fast. Each day the prelim and final swims got better as the week progressed. The swimmers gained momentum and confidence with each swim. This is a perfect example that a swimmer cannot believe what is in the heat sheet. All swimmers will have good swims and bad. I believe when it comes to looking at heat sheets they serve one purpose; which is to tell the swimmer heat and lane assignments. If coaches, parents, or swimmers start analyzing the heat sheet and talking to the swimmer about where they are seeded they impress the thought that the swimmer is only as good as what is in the heat sheet. When in reality they are much better than that if they are prepared to swim fast. The heat sheet can set a cap on what the swimmer believes to be true. It is part of the mental game of swimming, a trap not to fall into. The meet ended on a great note. Our girls medley relay set the national record from the consol heat solidifying our win in Long Beach. Looking at the heat sheet this group of swimmers were not seeded to win the meet. Through the team supporting each other and fast swims in prelims we were able to qualify for finals and create the win.

Junior National Team from 1993

Winning was the expectation at The Woodlands Swim Team, not only by the coaches but the swimmers as well. Swimmers started driving from other areas to become a part of our team. I believe in treating all swimmers the same, show no favoritism, live TEAM attitude then great things will happen. Fast swimming at Junior Nationals led to fast swimming at Senior Nationals and Olympic Trials. We placed in the top ten as a team at Senior Nationals as well as placed swimmers in the top eight at Olympic Trials for three consecutive trial meets.

The team and swimmer's success is ultimately the responsibility of the coach. A coach only needs a pool and motivation to create a successful team. Access to weights or a fifty meter pool can add to your program, but success can be achieved no matter the situation.

TEAM   67

As the coach you set the expectation for winning by creating a winning team attitude. By creating the workouts to get the swimmers to swim fast and creating the team atmosphere the coach sets the winning expectation. The second team I was a part of as the Head Age Group Coach won three consecutive Texas Age Group Championships training out of two twenty five yard high school pools. Winning is believing in each other and working together for a common cause.

Sometimes the swimmer is smarter than the coach. A coach must always listen to their swimmers. One year we attended a Senior National Meet in order to qualify for the U.S. National Team and the Pan Pac Games. The top two swimmers in each event qualified to represent the United States at the Pan Pac Games. Mathew Pierce was a swimmer of mine which I felt had a chance to make the team, he qualified fifth in prelims with his best time. One obstacle facing Matt in the finals of the 200 butterfly was the world record holder who was seeded first. Without asking for Mathew's input I instructed him on how to swim the race. The first words out of my mouth were to not go out with the world record holder. I instructed him to build pace on the first 50, maintain pace on the second and third 50's, and come home fast in the last 50. I was following a very common strategy for swimming a 200 meter swim. Instead Mathew went out tied with the world record holder at the first 50, was fourth at the 100 mark, fifth at the 150, at that point I threw my clipboard down and gave up on him. He came home in a :30 to out-split the world record holder on the last 50 and finished second, qualifying for the Pan Pac Games. From this experience I learned that there is no text book way for each swimmer to swim a race. Mathew Pierce taught me a valuable lesson that day; coaches should listen to their swimmers and learn from them just as they should learn from their coach. After that swim going forward I would sit with all my swimmers to listen to how they were feeling about the upcoming race. I always let my swimmers have a voice when it came to their individual swims. Coaches who think they know everything better be ready to reach into a bag of excuses. Mathew later went on to earn a scholarship to Stanford and win the 200 butterfly at the men's NCAA Championships.

Chapter 10

SWIM OFFS, DUAL MEETS, AND RELAYS

A few aspects of a swim season that come up will be swim offs and relays, but I made it a point to include dual meets as well. Not every swimmer will be in a swim off or relay, however they can be included in a dual meet. I felt dual meets were important to include in the season as an extra way to race events or to include different racing formats a swimmer may experience in the future. Relays are important for scoring points and always a highlight of swim meets. Relays are also the true example of TEAM. While having to swim a Swim off is not common, it will enable a swimmer to make it into the final heat and also score points.

SWIM OFFS

In the eighteen years I coached The Woodlands Swim Team, no swimmer to my knowledge ever lost a swim off. How can that happen? Team. I never agreed to a coin toss to solve a tie for eighth or sixteenth place. AAAO was the belief and attitude. Swim offs may mean the difference in making finals or going home. If a swimmer wins a swim off they are now in the finals earning valuable points for the team. These are difficult races for the swimmer because it is just two people swimming against each other. They are usually at the end of the day when people have left the pool and the energy in the room is fading. Even though swim offs do not happen often they are just as important as any other race at the meet. To combat the lower energy in the room our swimmers and parents made it a point to stay and cheer on the swimmer in the swim off. I feel this made a huge difference for the swimmer in the pool. Knowing the team was behind them and cheering them on to victory.

An example of one such swim off as told by Trent Trebona. At the time of the swim he was ten years old. Trent is currently the Head Age Group Coach for Mansfield Swim Team just outside of Dallas, Texas. I am proud after all these years to call him my friend…

SWIMMING FOR THE WOODLANDS SWIM TEAM:

One of my first, and maybe the most impactful, memories for me as an athlete on TWST was Age Group Champs at the old Alief pool. I was 9 years old. I had just moved from ATEX, so I had not been on the team for very long and swimming for TWST was a new experience.

I thought I knew, but I had no idea…I thought I knew what swimming on a team was all about until that Saturday at Alief.

I managed to get myself into a swim off in the 50 Fly. I did not think much of it—it was a 50 Fly against one other person after the prelim session was over and nobody would be around to see the outcome. Besides, I am just one of many kids on the team, if I do not win, no big deal.

Boy was I wrong.

The closer it got to the end of the prelim session, the more the natatorium started to empty out…except for TWST swimmers. It did not take long for me to realize why they were sticking around. Now I am feeling pressure. It had become abundantly clear that I was a part of something much bigger than myself and even the two laps I was about to swim.

As I find my way behind the blocks, I see a sea of green across the pool many teammates who I did not even know. Staying to watch me. To cheer for me. About that time, Coach Vogel walks up to me, looks me square in the eye, and tells me "TWST has never lost a swim off." Like John Wayne's first gun fight in "Red River," he was quick and direct with his message and then he walked to the side of the pool to watch the race.

I was nervous before, all of a sudden, I felt like I was about to lose control of my bowels...Was there any doubt who was going to win that race? No way was I going to let my teammates down or be the first to ever lose a swim off while wearing that prestigious green "W" on my cap.

I thought I knew, but I had no idea what the impact of a team could have on a swimmer.

—TRENT TRABONA
Head Age-Group Coach Mansfield Aquatic Club
TWST Swimmer 1990–2002
TWST Coach 2006–2014

This t-shirt was one of many we made for dual meets.

DUAL MEETS

Dual meets helped mold our team at The Woodlands. Each January the state of Texas scheduled double elimination dual meets for the ten best USA Swimming teams in Texas. These dual meets were set up collegiate style with collegiate team events. The teams could enter their top three swimmers for each event. I am very proud to say in my years coaching for The Woodlands we never lost a dual meet to another USA Swim Team. Team and AAA0 played a huge role in our success at these events. One of our goals at all meets was that nobody takes last place. I knew our best swimmers would handle their job, but we needed to give those zero points to the opposing team. I went so far as to bring along a coach whose entire responsibility was to scout the opposing teams. These meets were held at the Texas Swim Center with two meets running at the same time. This scout coach was in charge of watching the team we would face next. He was looking for who swam what event and their time. We would then look at the swims and make plans based on knowing the other team's strengths and weaknesses. This strategy was very beneficial, we knew the other team better than they knew us. I liked the collegiate format as it proved to be a good experience in preparing our swimmers for collegiate swimming. I also liked the experience the swimmers were gaining from dual meets so much that for a few years I would schedule a swim meet with a local university. These meets were a more mature environment to give swimmers an opportunity to swim older swimmers. I felt if my high school swimmers could swim against collegiate swimmers they would be better prepared to swim meets at the higher levels. I will always be thankful to these universities for helping our top swimmers prepare for elite competitions. One year we brought Texas A&M down to the last event. To accomplish a win we had to win the 200 breaststroke. Our breaststroker Clay Kennedy showed great courage facing the A&M All-American breaststroker. Dropping approximately five seconds off his time, Clay was able to get his hands to the wall first. Clay was a great team swimmer. I still tell his 200 breaststroke story to my swimmers today.

Texas A&M vs TWST

John Vogel was a pioneer in race strategies for age group swimming. We had such a tremendous roster with so much depth in every area. Our team meetings were led by John, but they were full of direction and input by the swimmers. TWST had a saying "big TEAM, little me". I recall preparing for a dual meet against a division I NCAA swim program. There was a collegiate All American 200 breaststroker on the opposing team and it was my job to take his points for TWST. I knew this was going to be a daunting task, but I was not willing to let my TEAM down. The 200 breast and 400 free relay are separated by less than

10 minutes in a College Dual Meet format. During our meet planning it was suggested by my teammates that I be placed on the 400 free relay. I bowed out as I knew that I would be gassed after the 200 breast and there were several swimmers that would have a better opportunity to assist us in our goals.

The energy on the deck during the 200 breaststroke was electrifying. The team was up and on deck and the noise was deafening. There is a certain peace that takes over once a race has begun. The ambient noise disappears, and the familiar focus of preparation takes over. As a sprinter, I was expected to be ahead in the first 100 and I was. John had modified my race strategy for this meet, and it was executed. The final lap was intense. Suddenly I could hear everything. My coach, my team, the fans, everything. We did not come to lose, and it was not going to be because of me.

TWST Attitude Era

There was something to be said for green and black. Our gear was a symbol of who we were. Champions. People knew that.

Consistency, dedication, and accountability are some of the attributes that TWST instilled in its athletes. We carry this forward in all aspects of life. There was a certain swagger to the Woodlands Swimmers. We were all champions, regardless of what the boards showed.

Accountability

There was a saying in the locker room, "what happens in the pool, stays in the pool". We pushed one another. There was so much talent on the team that the saying, iron sharpens iron, comes to mind. The workouts were difficult, but we all wanted to be there. There was a certain commitment to one another that kept us coming back.

Lasting Bonds

There is not a single TWST teammate that I would not meet with a smile and reminisce with, even after 30 years. I do not think there are any of us that feel differently.

Vogelisms

Simple, yet profound were these sayings. I still say them today. One example is when I have an arduous task in front of me. I will often mutter "well, it ain't gonna do itself". In my head I hear the familiar sharp-edged voice with a county drawl.

—CLAY KENNEDY
Past TWST swimmer

We also would swim dual meets with other USA Swim Teams. One year we hosted a dual meet for Dad's Club, a local team in Houston. At the time they had a great national reputation. Our swimmers seemed a little nervous going into the dual meet, so I wanted to create something big and crazy as a distraction for the swimmers. Something that was not part of our normal routine, it needed to be unexpected to change the mind's focus from concentrating on the nervousness. First we rented a smoke machine, and then I purchased a four foot boa constrictor. With the Dad's Club already in the stands, we went into our meeting room. The team knew something special was planned, just not what it was. While one coach set up the smoke machine another set up a loud speaker system. At the end of the meeting I reminded the team we did not have a mascot. With the swimmers pumped up I reached into my bag and pulled out the snake. The loud music and smoke machine began. As we walked out each swimmer touched our new mascot. With the song Welcome to My Nightmare by Alice Cooper playing, we walked to the end of the pool to do our team cheer. The atmosphere was electric; we won almost every event that day. Getting the swimmers pumped up and out of their heads by getting a little crazy actually works.

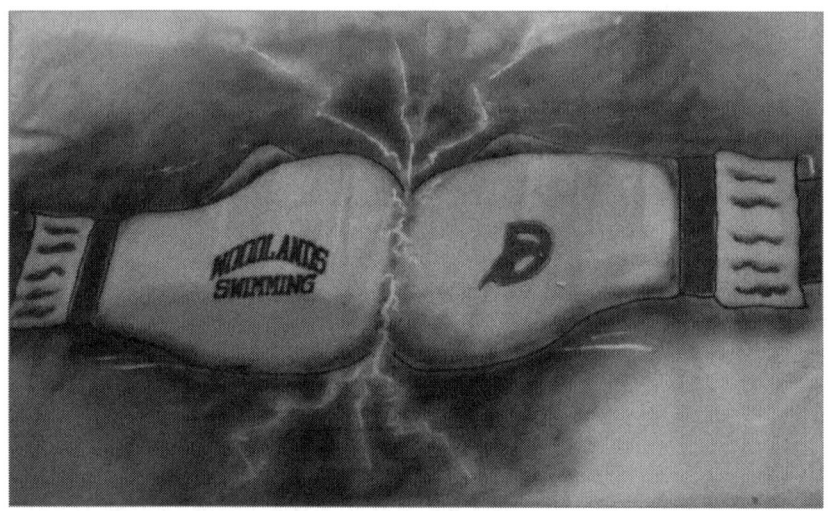

This is a banner from the dual meet against the Dad's Club.

RELAYS

When I think of relays I always think of double points, TEAM, and heart. Very seldom did the fastest swimmer anchor a relay, I anchored who I thought had the biggest heart. This swimmer showed consistency, did not think about the competition too much, and most importantly was willing to swim fast no matter the situation to touch the wall first. Our team won seven straight relays at long course Junior Nationals. All seven were anchored by TJ Fry. TJ was one of the most talented and toughest swimmers I had the privilege to coach…

As a young kid about 8 years old and fairly new at the sport of swimming, I was once placed on the anchor of a relay.

Both I and my coaches discovered quickly that the pressure and excitement of that 4th position did something to my performance. I can't put it clearly into words, but there's definitely a change when I would step up to anchor. I could physically feel it. From that point on I anchored nearly every relay I was put on for the next 15 years, from before the age of 10 through high school and college.

Some were more successful than others of course, but one particularly memorable race happened in Mission Viejo California in the finals of Junior Nationals West. I was swimming in the finals of the 400IM, which was immediately followed by the 800 freestyle relay. With only 1 heat of the female relay in between those two swims, I asked John not to be placed in the anchor position. I would be too tired to perform in that role. John agreed and said he would put in at the 2nd or 3rd leg.

My 400IM went well, but as I finished a quick warm down and joined the relay behind the blocks, John informed all us that I would anchor. Rightfully I was pissed that I had been lied to, but I understood the trick (to solely focus on the event in front of you and nothing else), so I accepted my fate.

We were the number one seed, but not by much. Our focus was on the second seed, Mission Viejo, but the reality of it was that there were 4 teams that could win this race. Our lead off, Jay Martin swam a brilliant leg and finished with a very slight lead over 4 other teams. Our second leg was Sean Galagher, who had finished second in the 200 freestyle earlier in the meet. Sean was able to build our lead and separate us a bit from the field. Our third leg was swam by Ed Nash. Ed was a strong freestyler, but was known for his breaststroke. Ed swam an amazing race, but as he headed for home, 3 other teams had closed the gap, with Mission Viejo, who was next to us, pulling about even.

I was tired from my 400 IM that I had swam only min-
utes prior, but like I mentioned earlier, something changes
when I step up to anchor a relay, like a switch turning on.
Mission Viejo's anchor was the 200 freestyle champion from
the meet, so I didn't have high hopes on the outcome of this
race. I was likely going to get out-muscled. My start was
better than his so I came up with a slight lead, but that
quickly evaporated as he quickly powered up and then past
me. I don't worry about the first 50 of a 200 on a relay as
adrenaline often plays a big role. The next 100 yards I swam
as close to his lane as possible to catch any draft and worked
to minimize his growing lead. By the third 50 he had stopped
pulling away, and by the turn for home I had actually made
up a little ground. In the final lap I laid it all out on the line.
I was either going to catch this guy or I was going to black
out. It started slowly at first, inching up from his ankles to
his knees, but as he began to fall apart from taking the race
out too fast, I began to close the gap quicker. With about 10
yards to go, the anchor for Mission Viejo had blown up and
I passed him in the final strokes to take back the lead and
continue The Woodlands Swim Team's undefeated streak.

—TJ FRY
Past TWST swimmer

Relays are an integral part of winning team championships, including the medal count at the Olympic games. Jason Lezak's anchor leg
at the Olympics running down the world record holder is a great
example of heart. You can also go back to the 1974 Olympics when
the American girls lost every individual event, yet won the 400
freestyle relay. How can that happen? Pride in the United States and
mentally preparing to bring home the win. These examples are two
of the biggest upsets in the history of the United States Swimming.

John Vogel

The following are a few entertaining relay stories. One year at a Gulf Champs meet our 400 freestyle relay was not seeded in the top three. According to the splits on paper we were definitely not supposed to win the race. Before the race I met with the boys and told them a story about a bear and a rabbit. A big burly bear and little white rabbit were walking through the woods together. The bear asked the rabbit "Does poop stick to your fur?" The rabbit perplexedly said "no." Then the bear walked up to the rabbit, picked him up, and wiped himself. The boys at this point were laughing and confused as to why I would tell them this story. Two reasons I told them this story. The first was for distraction. Secondly, I told the boys that lane four was the bear and they were the rabbit. I also told them to go prove lane four wrong. They won the relay, and later I asked them how they pulled the win off. In response the swimmers said they did not want to be the rabbit!

A second relay story occurred my freshman year at Tennessee; we had a dual meet at home against UCLA. The meet came down to the 400 freestyle relay. UCLA had their B team in the outside lane. We won a very close race. Once all the swimmers had finished the race, we headed for the pool to jump in and celebrate, but our coach forced us to back away from the pool. He was the only person that noticed UCLA's B team had gotten lapped on purpose and did a hand touch with 50 yards still to go. Had we entered the water we would have been disqualified. Relays can be tricky and it is the coach's responsibility to watch the entire relay race and not just the top couple of teams.

This third story is probably the most entertaining way to end a meet that I can remember. We were at one of those long open meets that lasted all day at an outdoor pool. Everyone had been in the hot sun all weekend and just wanted the meet to end. We had already won the meet, but a particular referee had been annoyingly watching our team the whole meet. During the last event he was judging the take offs in our lane of the girls 400 relay. I could not resist adding a little fun to the end of the meet. I told the head official what our relay was about to do. Our boy's captain put on a girl suit and swam third on the relay. It was absolutely hysterical and fun. The best part was the fact that this particular referee never noticed. Everyone at the meet had a good laugh except that referee. This was an example of adding a little fun and excitement to what had been a long weekend. Yes we gave up the points to the relay, but we had already won the meet. Everyone at the meet was able to enjoy the fun.

JULY 1986

These 15-16 year olds set two national relay records (400 medley, 3:28.64, 800 free, 6:52.58) at the All-American Meet: (clockwise) Brad Bailey, Todd Bartee; Jeff Thibault and Chris Cornman.

Interestingly, just a few years ago this same relay set a Master's record as men.

Some quick takeaways for success:

Don't lose swim offs…ever.

Swim dual meets every season

Make relays special all season for if you do, the relays will be there for you at the end of season

By training with AAA~~0~~ attitude, not backing down from swim offs or relays and scheduling collegiate format dual meets will prepare swimmers for success at any meet. Having the courage to be successful as a team will lead to individual success as well. Swim offs, dual meets, and relays all play a huge part of bringing the team together. Encouraging swimmers to have a little fun along the way also makes for a better TEAM. Coaches have the privilege of molding swimmers into incredible athletes. It takes courage from coaches, parents, and most of all swimmers to strive for success.

Chapter 11

EGO'S: USA SWIMMING VERSUS HIGH SCHOOL SWIMMING

have coached both high school as well as USA swimming teams. There are differences to coaching each one. However, coaching to be successful and swim fast is the goal for both.

First of all high school seasons are different in every state. For example, Florida's high school season ends in November, while in Texas the season ends in February. In the state of Texas, high school swimming is extremely competitive. Most every USA swimmer also swims high school as well. This is why it is imperative to work with the other coach to be able to maximize scholarship potential for the swimmer. It took me a few years to realize working with the high school coach was beneficial for both teams and the swimmer. Far too often conflicts in coaching methods arise between the two coaches while the athlete is put in the middle causing confusion. The "my swimmer/your swimmer" mentality can destroy two teams at the same time. Eventually the swimmer will have to choose between the two teams due to the coaches' egos. At times I've had swimmers from six to eight different high schools swim for The Woodlands Swim Team. There were several times dealing with multiple high school coaches was challenging. A mistake I made early on was telling a 1:38 200 yard freestyler and a twenty second 50 yard freestyler to not shave for their high school regional meet. This was before I understood how competitive the local high school swim teams were. I knew my swimmers were fast and thought they would have no problem qualifying for the state meet. Unfortunately, neither swimmer qualified for the state championship that year. I felt like the dumbest coach on the planet. After the meet, I told both swimmers as well as their high school coaches that it was my fault I interfered and it would never happen again. From this experience I learned we as coaches of both teams must work together.

Most college scholarships are solely based on time. It makes no difference if it occurs at a high school meet or a USA sanctioned meet. An exception to the rule are non-high school events. USA Swimming offers all competitive swimming events as does college swimming. Texas high school swimming offers a limited number of events, leaving out the 200 yard stroke distances, 400 individual medley, the 1000 and 1650 freestyle. This makes Texas high school swimming not ideal for the mid and long distance swimmers. Balancing decisions on resting and tapering for both high school and USA meets should be a collaboration so the swimmers swim the best at whichever meets are occurring. If a future scholarship is based on events not offered as a high school event, then both coaches must do what is best for the swimmer. Once the athletes' best interests are realized by both coaches, the swimmers on the team will embrace the decision knowing that both of their coaches are truly working together. Now we have achieved another definition of "oneness." Two teams, two coaches, and one swimmer working together.

> *John Vogel's teams always stood out at meets as being TEAMS. He brought a radical idea into what was always believed to be an individual sport: that when people connect to a single mission or identity, incredible potential is unlocked and realized. His teams knew this secret and he was a master at creating that reality for them.*

> —MATT KREDICH
> Men's and Women's Head Coach University of Tennessee

Chapter 12

KENNY

learned early on the importance of diving if you want to win high school or college meets. At the University of Tennessee under the guidance of coach Vince Panzano, the diving team was a significant part of our team success. The divers cared about the swimmers and the swimmers encouraged the diving team.

One summer I was coaching a Woodlands swim practice when I saw the arrival of the new diving coach, Kenny Armstrong, a three time Olympic diver and six time Olympic diving coach. He was wearing a Mission Bay t-shirt to his first diving practice, rookie mistake...so I thought. As the divers gathered around to meet their new coach, Kenny removed the Mission Bay shirt, pulled out a can of lighter fluid and burned the shirt to the applause of the team. As he put on a Woodlands Diving shirt I gained an immediate respect for him. I have been fortunate to call him my friend for thirty years.

*John and Kenny Armstrong at the Texas Swimming and
Diving Hall of Fame ceremony after accepting the Wally Pryor
Distinguished Team award for The Woodlands Swim Team.*

Several times over the years Kenny has helped my swimmers with
their starts. He was able to work the swimmers by explaining proper
water entry angles to achieve the best depth under the water for
racing. Too shallow is not ideal because of surface tension at the
point where air and water meet. If the entry is too deep then the
distance to break the surface is too far to accomplish with speed.
At the perfect angle the swimmer breaks the surface of the water at
maximum race speed. Having Kenny working with the swimmers
on form and body position entering the water definitely gave my
swimmers an advantage on their starts.

The year I coached the high school team we won the Texas State
Championship because of valuable points produced by the diving
team. We won the meet together, swimmers, divers, and parents
as a team. Embracing the diving team as part of the team will lead
to total team success.

I started coaching at The Woodlands in the fall of 1989. I had been there one time before when I was the coach for the Canadian World Cup team in 1982 (I think that was the year). We were billeted at homes within The Woodlands back when it used to feel like family!

I looked around at that meet and told myself that I would be coaching here one day. Low and behold the lord blessed me with the opportunity and 7 years later my dream came true!

I arrived here from Mission Bay Florida where I had been Ron O'brien's assistant coach. I loved every moment of learning from the best coach in the world at the time, but I needed to branch out on my own and jumped at the opportunity.

When I first got here there were 11 kids on the team after 1 week there were 5 left. My contract was for a whopping $16,000.00/ year and my boss told me do not ask for a raise because you won't get one he said. So I figured I might as well coach the ones that would listen because it didn't matter to my income whether there was 1 or 100 on the team so we set out at that time to get as good as we could.

We ended up doing pretty well overall and I've loved every minute of coaching in The Woodlands for the past thirty years.

I'm so happy Vogel has decided to write this book and tell his story of coaching swimming. I've never been a huge fan of swimming usually because every program that I've been involved with has to take a back seat because they are the biggest lobbying group in any facility. But for some reason Vogel and I hit it off right from the start. Probably because I totally respected how his college coach approached the sport. John definitely has a little coach Bussard in him.

He is the epitome of TEAM. He lived it, loved it and coached it better than most and I'm privileged to call him one of my best friends.

Enjoy this book, I know I will.

—KENNY ARMSTRONG
Coach of The Woodlands Diving Academy
Six Time Olympic Diving Coach
Two Time Olympic Diver

Most USA swim teams do not have the experience of competing alongside a diving team. I was fortunate at The Woodlands to have Kenny. However, swimmers will have the opportunity to compete on a team with divers on high school and collegiate teams. As a coach I took the opportunity to gain valuable knowledge from Kenny and worked together with him to help the swimmers improve. Sometimes a start entry makes all the difference in the world in a race that could come down to hundredths of a second. Capitalizing on gaining knowledge from the people around you will lead to success in swimming and your personal life. I was lucky to have Kenny as part of The Woodlands and to also call him a good friend for over thirty years.

*A picture of Laura Wilkinson and Kenny
at the 2008 Olympics in Beijing.*

Chapter 13

COLLEGE

U p to this point in a swimmer's life choosing a university is one of the biggest decisions a swimmer and family is going to make. During the recruiting process it is important to remember your choice in universities is not just about swimming. The university the swimmer chooses will greatly influence their future with the degree they earned. No matter the sport, at the collegiate level you are considered a "student athlete". In order to make this process smoother I would meet with the senior swimmer and their family in the fall. I wanted to be sure the family was prepared with knowledge about the process and points to consider before decisions had to be made. However, with current NCAA rules I believe these discussions should be their Junior year of high school, not senior year. In our meeting we went over five consideration points. The points to take into account are location, budget, future education level, prospective coach, and size of the university.

The first criteria to think about is how the location of the college could play a role in the swimmer's future. One thing to consider is the weather in the location of the university. I once had a swimmer who had lived in Texas his entire life attend Harvard on a scholarship. I do not think Jay Martin ever got used to those cold winters in Massachusetts. Also will the swimmer prefer to live close or far from home and family. Will your swimmer want to come home more often or maybe just during winter break? Some swimmers want to be located close to home in order to see family more often. Perhaps the parents want to attend swim meets and football games.

Budget plays a role here because the cost and time to travel home each time will need to be considered. For some families location is not a factor leaving options open to the swimmer. The last point to think about here is in some cases the location of a university leads to more than just a four year decision. I have had swimmers attend UCLA, Stanford, and USC which upon graduating many stayed in California. Everything from job offers to relationships which happen over the course of university life can influence their swimming careers or post collegiate decisions.

The second and third criteria are budget and the education the swimmer desires for the future. I put these together because these factors go hand in hand. The future education needed for a career may be influenced by what education programs are offered to students. This in turn may narrow down choices for the swimmer and influence the budget. Family income and situation are probably the most important factors to consider when choosing a college. Other family members are important to keep in mind and timing of those members going to college. Scholarships options for them will also be part of the budget to take into consideration. College costs differ a great deal from one to another private, in-state or out of state all come with different price tags, and not everyone is offered a full scholarship. The family should know scholarships offered vary in dollar amount and are only offered one year at a time.

Something else to think about should be injuries or life changes. A swimmer is not immune to injury. A swimmer can sustain an injury which may require surgery and an intensive long road to recovery. This may even be a swimming career ending injury, but the swimmer would like to remain at the school. Likewise, life happens during the years at a university. Perhaps the athlete's life goals change where swimming is no longer the priority. Marriages and careers can begin during this time changing the direction from where the athlete started. Can the family afford to pay the cost of the school if the swimmer no longer has a scholarship to help offset the cost? A student athlete must manage proper balance between the degree they want while taking into consideration what is financially possible for the family.

The fourth point to consider is the perspective coach. The coach can personally help the swimmer not only become a better athlete, but influence life choices as well. I have stayed in contact with many of my coaches for years after my own swimming career ended. When I arrived at the University of Tennessee, I was an only child whose only care in life was how fast I was swimming. I did many things wrong my freshman year, but Coach Bussard was tough. He showed no favoritism, but most importantly he taught me perseverance and "oneness". This has been with me my entire life, and I have always tried to instill these values in my swimmers. In selecting a school to attend, finding the right fit for you is more important than the size of scholarship. College teams have a limited amount of scholarships. The scholarships may be split up into room and board, books and tuition. The college coach has a great responsibility to recruit the right athletes that fit his or her team needs. With limited scholarships, many times they will fill the team where they are weak. College coaches prefer offering scholarships to swimmers who double as relay swimmers to score extra points while adding depth to the team. The coach has to trust the swimmers to perform both in the classroom as well as in the pool. While the swimmer has to trust the coach to support him in training to continue success in the sport. The coach and swimmer relationship must complement each other in order to build a successful team.

Finally, the fifth point to consider is whether the swimmer wants to be a big fish in a little pond or a small fish in a big pond. Winning teams are going to demand and expect more from their swimmers. I always encourage a minimum of five visits to different colleges that meet the swimmer and family's needs. Visiting a variety of universities that meet the family criteria will give the swimmer perspective on university life. Large universities may have more to offer, but a small school may fit the swimmer's personality better. Larger universities have much larger classes and social circles. A smaller university which has smaller class sizes may be more beneficial for the student. Remember a swimmer is a student first. Once the visits are completed, your heart will tell you where you belong. The collegiate experience in most cases will be the memories and stories you share for the rest of your life.

When I was looking at universities my top choice was SMU. I had wanted to go there for a long time as they had a top notch swim team. My mother on the other hand wanted me to attend college somewhere different. I told the SMU coach, George McMillion I wanted to swim there but my mother had problems with that. The following week the coach came down to Houston for a visit with my parents. He said all the things parents want to hear. I told him while he was there that I was ready to sign the papers, but he said I should wait and finish my recruiting visits. The final trip was to the University of Tennessee, and I fell in love. I loved the campus, but more importantly the closeness of the swimmers on the team. I particularly loved the way the team culture was so important. I loved it so much that I signed the papers before I left to go home. My mother was so upset she took my car away for a year and the promise of one hundred acres of land she was going to buy for me. The decision to attend the University of Tennessee changed the rest of my life. It shaped me into the man I became, and the way I coached swimmers the rest of my career.

John Vogel during his freshman year at the University of Tennessee

Now that the swimmer has left and spent a semester at school the next thing to think about will be winter and summer break training. Most swimmers I coached would come home and train at The Woodlands during winter break. This is a short time period and swimming at home is the most convenient option. However, during the summer the time frame is much longer and a swimmer has options. They can stay at the university if a summer program is offered or come home. If your USA swim team has provided a program you have trusted and excelled in, coming home for summer training will be a great experience for both swimmers and the USA swim coach. Sharing experiences and knowledge with your teammates should also be welcomed and appreciated. I encouraged our college swimmers to not only come home to train in the summer but also bring a friend. Family's seemed to welcome these swimmers by housing them. The experience level they brought to our team was priceless. Post college swimmers that wish to continue their swimming career after college normally have the choice of training with their home USA team, another USA team, or sometimes their college team. One such example we had at The Woodlands was a LSU graduate, Adam Schmitt. He came back home to train at The Woodlands Swim Team for two years to prepare for Olympic trials. Because of excellent training under head coach Dr. Sam Freas, Adam had become a great sprinter for our USA National Team. Both Adam as well as Sam greatly influenced our sprint program at The Woodlands. Adam brought back with him techniques he had learned from Sam and I was able to implement some of them for the younger swimmers.

It was the summer of 1992 and I was preparing for the US Olympic Trials. The team was all going to their different championship meets but I was the lone Trial qualifier for TWST. Of course, I was the older post grad guy that swam mostly on his own but to me there was always a sense of team spirit. As Trials arrived, I will never forget the support I received from the entire team, departing and returning with a hero's welcome. That doesn't come naturally, young swimmers just don't go to the airport to cheer on their team-

mate without great guidance and having been taught this important tenet of a great team: Support and Pride! Sure, I have swam on many US National Teams and traveled around the world to meets but I never have experienced such a genuine display of support and pride in all my swimming career. I will always remember these moments and I do believe it is an integral part of developing a swim TEAM.

—ADAM SCHMITT
Former USA National Team member and
NCAA Collegiate coach.
Currently Fulshear Racing Swim Team.

Adam Schmitt at the team send off for Olympic Trials in 1992

Location, budget, future education, the coach, and size of the university are only some of the examples to take into consideration when choosing a university. These are what I consider the big five, but each family is different and will have other criteria to consider as well. The point is to communicate with each other as a team to make the best choice for the swimmer and family. After the parameters for choosing are set the swimmer should take their visits and make the best choice for them. College swimming will provide many memorable experiences. I know for me it has influenced not only my swimming career, but my coaching career as well.

John Vogel

Chapter 14

NEVER SAY NEVER

Front page from Texas Swim Magazine when John retired.

When I retired from coaching and bought a business, the long time University of Texas coach, Eddie Reese called and asked me if I thought I would miss coaching and eventually coach again. I answered never again, I felt I had achieved my goals. His response was "never say never". However, after fifteen years in the business of selling swim suits and equipment, I realized I missed working on the pool deck. A great deal had changed in fifteen years in swimming. Theories, training techniques, and technology were just a few points I had to catch up on. I also realized some of the things we did at The Woodlands Swim Team would not work with today's swimmer, not to mention the rule changes. I reached out to coaches who were still coaching and did research to get caught up to the current world of swimming.

After a year giving private lessons to adult fitness swimmers and triathletes I was offered a part time job with a small swim team. At first I was asked to coach the senior level sprinters twice a week. I certainly had no aspirations to be a head coach again, yet enjoyed being able to help swimmers. It felt great being back on the pool deck again and after one season was offered the head coaching position. After declining the position, I was given the entire senior group. I coached four days a week with no responsibility to attend the meets, it was a perfect fit for me. Fortunately one of my retired swimmers was hired for the title of Head Coach, Trent Trebona. Together we were able to infuse the TEAM aspect. With Trent on board, the team received the Horizon Award," most improved team in Texas" at TAGS.

The team had a few promising swimmers, but as many teams with a great deal of swimmers, many more were overlooked. Concentrating on only the fastest swimmers leaves the rest of swimmers without direction. This way of thinking will not create successful swimmers or teams. A team includes everyone in the pool, on the pool deck, as well parents. It takes all the pieces of the team working together to be successful. My thinking has always been to coach everyone in the pool to achieve goals which in turn will inspire everyone to become better athletes.

I was frustrated with the fact that the goals of all the swimmers were not taken into account. I wanted the slower swimmers to know they mattered just as much as anyone else in the pool. I decided to take over these lanes leaving the faster swimmers to Trent. These swimmers had not been held accountable or given direction on how to improve. In my opinion they had gotten little attention. They just swam up and down the lanes in a train. After observing them at practice I noticed they would miss intervals no matter what the intervals were. At the time I took over the lanes, these swimmers reminded me of amoebas. I knew that my time with the team was limited, yet felt obligated to help inspire this group of swimmers to be better. I spoke with the swimmers in this lane and asked them what their goals were. One girl said her goal was to break a minute in the 100 freestyle, her best time so far had been 1:02. I believe if that had remained her goal, she would swim a minute plus for the next couple of seasons. We had a long chat, and I told her a story about a boy who collected fleas. As the boy caught fleas he would put them in a glass container which he called his flea circus. After several weeks of watching the fleas jump up and bang their heads into the lid he believed they were so well trained they would not jump any higher than the lip of the lid. He could remove the lid and the fleas stayed inside not jumping any higher than the lip of the jar. We talked about the minute mark as being the lid. Once she decided to take the lid off her goal of breaking the minute mark, she swam a 57.4 at the next meet. Giving a little time and attention to these swimmers helped them see they could be successful swimmers and improve their swimming.

This also reminds me of a story about rats which illustrates this point perfectly. I am not smart enough to come up with this one, yet Lanny Lanthrop, Texas High School Hall of Fame coach told this story at an ASCA clinic. I will try and give it the justice it deserves. A scientific experiment was conducted at a major university involving three rats and three students. The goal was for the rats to make their way through a maze for a reward of food at the end. For the sake of this story, think of the students as coaches. Rat number one was considered a very smart rat who would be able to find his way out of the maze and get his food. The coach of rat number two was told this was a semi smart rat and may or may not get through the maze. The coach of rat number three was told this rat was stupid and would never see the end of the maze. As the coaches left to train their rats, they had already formed conclusions of the rat's abilities. After months of training, the day finally came to see the results. Rat one achieved immediate success, rat two struggled for a while but succeeded, and rat three never found his way out of the maze. The truth was there was not a smart, average or stupid rat. All the rats' intelligence were the same but because of the coaches preconceived ideas the rats were trained as such. If each rat had been trained as though they could finish the maze each rat would have achieved the goal of finishing the maze. As coaches we must give each swimmer equal attention and not put limits to the success of any swimmer. Swimmers at any ability level can and should have goals. Encouraging all swimmers on a team to be successful will only add to the team culture. Swimmers in lane eight can and will produce a diamond or two and will make a difference in the team score.

After a short time Trent left the team and is currently a very successful Head Age Group Coach in Mansville, Texas. I felt that I had done the best job I could with this program and felt it was time to move on, retiring once again. "Never say never."

Months later I was approached by a swim parent with a ten year old daughter, Sarah, who wanted private lessons. Having not worked with age group swimmers for so long I felt it would not be a good experience; so I declined. After several conversations with this persistent parent, I agreed to one free lesson. In my head I did not want these lessons to continue forward. I was retired. I had not worked with age group swimmers in years, they are a different type of swimmer whose needs are different than senior level swimmers. I was not sure I would be able to relate to such a young swimmer one on one. Before the meeting arrived I had convinced myself this was not going to work. I wanted to get the lesson over with and move on with my retired life. I started the lesson without introducing myself and told her to go swim a twenty five yard freestyle without breathing. Her reply, "I can't do that." I went from wanting to get out of the lesson to accepting a challenge. I decided to have a restart of the lesson. We sat and talked for about fifteen minutes. We talked about many things, everything from her favorite food to her favorite movie. As we established a relationship and trust I told her to think about how that movie ended and swim the twenty five without breathing. She agreed to try. She did it easily and surfaced with a big smile. I was able to get to know Sarah a little bit more and as she relaxed was able to complete the twenty-five. Once trust is established the swimmer will start to believe in themselves and great things begin to happen. I have now worked with her for five years and added ten to twelve other kids as well to my lesson program. Sarah, along with Eddie Reese, taught me to "never say never." By the way, she dropped over ten seconds the first season I worked with her and won the 200 individual medley at TAGS.

I met Coach Vogel when I was ten years old. I had just started club swimming about a year prior and had enjoyed a little success. I was hooked on it, the water felt like home. Now five years later, I have had more successes and a lot of failures and Coach Vogel has been a huge part of it all. From day one he was always pushing me to be the best I could be and in the time I have spent learning from him, I have learned how to be a better swimmer and teammate. He has shown me how to have fast times and leadership qualities without sacrificing any part of who I am. He has cared about each of us, his lesson kids, as individuals and without even desiring to do so, he built us into our own sort of team. Coach Vogel is the kind of coach that commands your attention and respect through his confidence, knowledge and ability to care about each swimmer as an individual. And it shows. It shows in our swimming and in our life. I could never be thankful enough for all he has given me.

—SARA CULBERSON
Current lesson swimmer

Two years ago I had the pleasure of meeting a very unique young man with an amazing swimming talent, Munzy Kabbara. At the time he was struggling a bit with swimming. He was not dropping time anymore and felt stagnant in the water. He compared to being in a rut. Munzy had big goals he wanted to achieve. After we met for a couple of lessons, I realized just how talented he is. Munzy has dual citizenship in the United States and Lebanon. Boy, I had much to learn as I was not familiar with any cultural traditions in Lebanon. Throughout the first year working with him I learned everything from the Olympic swimmer selection process in Lebanon to Ramadan. His training had to be adjusted to accommodate his lifestyle; what a challenge. Working closely with his family, we came up with a plan to maximize his training. His success over the last year has been outstanding due to the collaboration with his USA swim team coach as well as Munzy's great work ethic. He is now considered to be one of Lebanon's top choices to make the next Olympic Games. Munzy just committed to a university in Texas to further his swimming career and Olympic dreams. I am proud he continues to encourage all of the lesson group swimmers to achieve their goals by words of encouragement and leading by example. Even in a group of swimmers from several different teams they are brought together as one. This group encourages and cheers each other on at meets as their own team. I truly believe Munzy will achieve his goal of swimming at the next Olympic Games.

Anyone who knows him will say that Coach Vogel is one of the most knowledgeable swim coaches to ever train swimmers, but his true brilliance is demonstrated by his decades of openness to uninterrupted learning and how he sees the idea of TEAM. Because of his attention to individualized physical and mental excellence, each athlete who listens to him is the best version of themselves and ready to be a successful team member."

—MUNZY KABBARA
FLEET Junior National Medalist,
Lebanese National Record holder and
Texas A&M Swim and Dive commit in the class of 2025

What started with a ten year old girl wanting a lesson to a potential Olympic swimmer and other swimmers in between accomplishing their goals, I have learned a great deal. Building Team into a group of swimmers from different teams has been challenging but so rewarding. I love working with these athletes. "Never say never" took on a whole new meaning for me. My message to swimmers is never be an amoeba, and to coaches do not train swimmers as rats. Build Team culture and principles into your program and your swimmers will thrive.

Chapter 15

LITTLE THINGS
BIG RESULTS

Taking ownership of training is up to the swimmer. Responsibility of applying the techniques the coach teaches lies solely with the swimmer. Coaches can teach all the techniques out there in the swimming world, but if the swimmer does not believe in or apply the techniques the swimmer will not be the best he or she can be. Showing up is simply not good enough if you want to be a top level swimmer. Capitalizing and applying training techniques by swimming fast at practice during tough sets everyday with every stroke will propel the swimmer to the next level.

As swimmers age and move up levels they should be less dependent on their parents. It is up to the swimmer to be part of the discussions about what events to swim at a meet and the reasons behind those decisions. Taking ownership over their own swimming by being prepared to swim their races at meets by knowing breathing patterns, dolphin kicks, and stroke counts is the responsibility of the swimmer. Essentially swimming a race should be on auto pilot because the swimmer is prepared. The more the swimmer trains these points in practice, it will lead to better success during the race. Training the little things in practice to a point in which muscle memory takes over and becomes part of the swim. Thinking about those little things distracts from the goal of swimming fast. When a coach starts reminding swimmers how many breaths to take, how many strokes, and all the little things that happen during a race the swimmer walks to the blocks distracted. Swimmers should arrive at the blocks with a clear mind ready to race.

An important aspect of any race is the dolphin kicking off the start and walls after a turn. Dolphin kicking starts the pace and breathing patterns for the race. If not done properly during practice, the swimmer will not do them correctly during a race. This takes training and muscle memory to be effective during a race. Kicks should come so naturally that the swimmer is not thinking about them during the race. Different events will dictate the proper number of underwater dolphin kicks for each individual. The number of kicks can and will affect breathing patterns during the race leading a swimmer to ask, "how do breathing patterns affect my race and performance during a race?" The answer is complicated and comes down to different types of muscle structure. The short answer for swimmers is some racers require more oxygen in their body to maintain speed and endurance while others require less. Proper oxygen levels for peak performance are influenced by muscle structure and training habits. A coach does not swim the race, but prepares swimmers during practices to ensure success. Race success ultimately comes down to the athlete taking ownership of training the little things during swim practice. The little things should be addressed in practices by the coach by teaching the swimmer to know their dolphin kicks and breathing patterns. Creating an environment of learning and responsibility leads to individual and team success.

A second aspect of training the little things is breath control while underwater kicking. The very first element is safety, most importantly not hyperventilating before practicing underwater breathing sets. Underwater training is a long term commitment that builds upon itself and will take months for the body to adapt. The swimmer must know their body and be able to communicate with the coach. You cannot expect success in the beginning, you must take baby steps to increase lung capacity by working on it daily. Dolphin kicking underwater is completely counterproductive if it is not faster than swimming. Although for many, if not most, dolphin kicking is faster and should be encouraged. Once you establish which is faster, you are off and running with your daily practices to embrace what you need to train. If dolphin kicking is faster, you must train breath control safely over a long period of time.

Now once the swimmer has established how far he can go underwater at a speed faster than swimming using strokes. Breathing patterns must be addressed for that particular event. I have noticed lately that many world class swimmers have increased the number of breaths taken during each length of the pool, especially in the 200 butterfly and 400 individual medley, yet they keep their underwater dolphin kick count consistent. Few swimmers will like or embrace this type of swimming. When first introduced they have to be convinced to try to move forward underwater because the natural inclination is to swim on the surface. Dolphin kicking at two feet underwater in a streamlined body position is faster than swimming on the surface for most swimmers. Underwater training must be done faster than race speed to capitalize on this technique; otherwise this will not be the most efficient during a race. I had the privilege to coach a great swimmer, Jeff Thibault. He could kick underwater very fast, faster than most could swim, including himself. At the state meet his senior year Jeff won the 100 backstroke taking only three strokes. It took Jeff two years of training in order to achieve this. This was before the fifteen meter rule was in effect. "If you believe it, you can achieve it."

The main responsibility a coach has to a swimmer is to teach and train techniques to allow the swimmer to improve and swim fast. In return a swimmer must believe in the training and techniques, apply them by taking ownership of his own swimming. Communication between coach and swimmer is paramount. A team environment allows for this communication which leads to greater success in and out of the pool.

"The only place success comes before work is in the dictionary" (Vince Lombardi).

Chapter 16

SUPPORT CREW

Coaching Staff, Board Members, and Parents

There are many people involved within a team which can influence the successes or failures of the team. A team consists of a head coach, head age group coach, assistant coaches, board of directors, parents, and most importantly the swimmers. Also, I was blessed to have an administrative person to handle meet entries, transportation, and other office duties. She was responsible for entering all the paperwork for swim meets. When all of these individuals work together as one, success will become part of the team's culture.

HEAD COACHES:

Even though the head coach speaks for the staff, he must take the staff's words with the utmost respect. Trust, loyalty, and respect must be shared and encouraged by the head coach and his staff. Head coaches cannot expect athletes to believe in Team if the staff does not believe the same. We would have regular staff meetings where we might have disagreements, but we would talk issues out. We respected each other and each other's opinions so that we were able to discuss situations to come together in agreement. We always left those meetings together on the same page supporting each other. We were a team. Head Coaches give your staff credit for team accomplishments while taking responsibility for failures, and the loyalty will follow. Remember the staff is setting the example for the team to follow, as are you.

HEAD AGE GROUP COACH

I believe the head age group coach is the most important ingredient on the staff. I believe at The Woodlands I had the very best. This person not only needs to be a great coach, but also share the goal of the entire team succeeding. Their role is to bring together age group swimmers to inspire them to work together as one, teach what is expected of them, and how important their role is to the team. The head age group coach is also instrumental in teaching proper swimming techniques so that as a swimmer ages success will follow.

Joel Engle on the pool deck at The Woodlands Athletic Club

John Vogel

I was blessed to work with what I believe to be the best age group coach for my first thirteen years at The Woodlands Swim Team. I would like to give credit to much of our age group success to Head Age Group Coach, Joel Engle. He deserves as much credit for winning as I do. He supported the team mentality and together we had a truly awesome team culture. He related to the age group swimmers and they loved swimming for him. He was key in bringing TEAM to the age group swimmers and bringing the age group swimmers to TEAM. Unfortunately for personal reasons, Joel was unable to attend his last TAGS meet. The swimmers and parents were so disappointed to have to attend TAGS without Joel, some were ready to walk out. I called a parent meeting to rally the parents to be there for their swimmers who had been working so hard that season. With the parents on board they went all in making signs and rallying behind the swimmers. With one coach gone, another in the hospital having a baby, and my last coach ill in the hospital, I was the only coach left to be there for all the swimmers at the TAGS meet that year. Luckily, a few other coaches from other teams volunteered to help me coach the age group swimmers. I am grateful for all the help and support the team received during the meet. Here are a few words from one of the coaches which helped that meet.

> *John Vogel made all of us better coaches. We had to be. No matter how fast we got our swimmers to go, there were always going to at least two, sometimes three or four TWST swimmers they had to race.*
>
> *John and I didn't like each other. There were times we would be standing next to each other on deck each ignoring the other, literally two feet apart.*
>
> *When I walked up to John's office, he had several other coaches inside, there to help him and TWST at TAGS. I walked in and said "I'm not doing this for you, this is for*

Joel, I still don't like you, but give me a damn shirt and let's go." Thanks,

—PATRICK HENRY
CEO Swim Coach Staffing Solutions

After this meet, I was in need of a Head Age Group Coach. I hired Tim Bauer. He remained Head Age Group Coach for five years as the team continued achieving success. After I retired in 1997, Tim became the Head Coach of The Woodlands Swim Team.

ASSISTANT COACHES:

The size of the team usually dictates how many assistants a team has on staff. Again these coaches must believe in the team goals in order to encourage the swimmers daily to achieve these goals. Assistant coaches must be loyal to the head coach and head age group coach to support TEAM culture. Many times I felt as if they were a part of my family. As our team began to win more meets, the bond between our staff just grew stronger. As swimmers moved up to different group levels as well as to different coaches, the past coach embraced and encouraged the move. The coaches did not have a my swimmer/your swimmer mentality. We were all The Woodlands Swim Team. At the Woodlands when a swimmer qualified for a national level meet, they received the teams' national swimming shirt, swimming cap, and were celebrated by all the coaches.

"It is amazing how much can be accomplished when no one cares who gets the credit" (Harry S. Truman and John Wooden).

BOARD MEMBERS

Board members can be a coach's best friend or worst enemy. Teams that are governed by a board of directors face many challenges, all of which can be overcome and transitioned into success by working together. I believe the head coach must have a position on the board of directors because the head coach has the greatest input for representing the team and swimmers. During board meetings I would give the status of the team. What does this mean? I would inform the board of the schedule of events for the calendar which included swim meets the team would be attending, dual meets, championship meets, and national meets. I also looked for when any team functions would fit in the schedule. I also discussed when selections for relays would be made and requested any items the team may need such as t-shirts or caps. A rule I had regarding board meetings was that coaching of swimmers could not be on the agenda. There is a time and place for those discussions after practice. The swim coach should not tell a board member how to do their job outside of swimming, just as they should not tell the coach how to coach.

The Board's main function is to manage and raise funds, facilitate trips to meets and plan team functions. The Board Members also played an integral part in supporting swimmers at swim meets. At the TAGS meet the Board would create inspirational posters for each child and hang them on their hotel doors. Boards can be a major part of a team's success or become part of their failure. I never missed a board meeting, and I never socially interacted with them outside of our team. I tried to keep it professional and not become friends. Coaches and Board Members each have different responsibilities to the team but work closely together to do great things. We had a wonderful Board of Directors, especially at The Woodlands, they were definitely part of TEAM.

SWIM PARENTS

Parents have a powerful impact on the team. Parents are board members, volunteers, swim officials, cheerleaders, and chauffeurs. They also plan and host team events outside the pool such as team movie nights and banquets. Their support toward the whole team's success moves mountains. For a team to be successful, the parents must also believe in the team's goals and success for all the swimmers. Negativity by parents does not help build the team culture, it works against it. Success cannot be achieved when negativity by parents undermines the hard work done by the swimmers and coaches. No one on the team is more important than anyone else. TEAM is a family of swimmers, coaches, and parents who work together to accomplish goals. When swimmers still communicate with the coach twenty or thirty years later, this is the success of TEAM and as a coach you have done your job. You have created a lifelong bond with these swimmers. Parents participation and encouragement helps solidify the team and sets an example for swimmers to follow.

> *I find it humorous that John would ask me to write about parents because he and I didn't really see eye to eye on parent/coach relationships. While we agree on 99.9% of other coaching aspects we didn't agree on the parent/coach relationships. I enjoyed becoming friends with parents on the team. While John would never believe me I don't think it ever interfered with my coaching. I did get my feelings hurt numerous times, but I think it was worth it because I learned valuable lessons. I can tell you this much, some of those parents are still my best friends 20 years later and I cannot imagine my life without them. They are still considered part of my family. Parents can be tough but all coaches know that they are an important part of what we do. Without the parents support we would have no swimmers attending practice, volunteers to run meets or to officiate. We have to have their trust and support to run the team. They are part of the FAMILY!*
>
> *I like to think that since I have been a parent of swimmers I can see things through a parent's eyes. I made several*

huge mistakes as a swimming parent so I can understand where parents are coming from and what they are going through when they are out of line. I often tell them they can never surprise me because I have been there and done that. What parents really want are for things to be fair, they want their swimmer to be important to the coach, and they want them to enjoy the adventure. It's not an easy task but sometimes looking at it from a parents point of view is the most important thing we can do as coaches.

—COACH SHANA TRABONA
Coached at The Woodlands Swim Team from 1989 to 2015.
Numerous state championships, top 10 swimmers
and national record holders.

As important as swim parents are to the organization and the team, I always felt apprehensive getting too close to parents. I wanted to protect the team from favoritism. I looked at it as if I went to one graduation, I had to attend them all. I felt it important to not show favoritism to one swimmer over another. I was the coach and they were the swimmers. The only exception I made was to attend funerals to support and pay respect to the family, and sadly there were a few. I had strict rules for the parents on the team. Parents were allowed to watch workouts, but were not allowed to talk with coaches during practice. I always made sure coaches were available after practice for face to face conversations. There had to be clear boundaries between parents and coaches, just as there are between parents and teachers at school. I always told my swimmers "I am not your parent, I am not your friend, I am not here to hang out with, I am your coach."

Throughout my years coaching I am proud to say I worked with amazing people. The drive for success could not have been accomplished without them. I am honored to say I still have many swimmers, who are now well into adulthood, call me to talk about events in their lives. I now consider them my friends as well as extended family. When head coaches, assistant coaches, board members, and parents work together as one to strive towards a common goal it is amazing what can be accomplished, Team.

Chapter 17

COWBOY UP

Building a Team

hate to lose more than I like to win. If coaches, swimmers and parents can embrace that thought as a team, great results will happen. "There is no I in team."

Fox Den Country Club in Knoxville, Tennessee was my first coaching job. Just one summer with a summer league team. The summer before, the team had lost every dual meet. Working with my friend and head coach instilling team concepts we went undefeated that summer. This was my first introduction as a coach on how a team mentality can affect results.

My second coaching job was for Meyerland Swim Team. One of my high school coaches Pete Payne, who is also a Texas Swimming and Diving Hall of Fame inductee, encouraged me to move from Knoxville to Houston to be his assistant coach. Shortly after I took the position Pete left the team. All of a sudden I found myself head coach for the first time. Applying my limited knowledge about TEAM, I started to see how the swimmers responded. They swam for not only themselves but each other. After just one season a team was born, and we finished seventh at the Texas Age Group State Championships.

At that time I began to talk with successful coaches in our sport about the strength of team concepts and how it affects results. I learned a successful team not only includes all swimmers and coaches but the parents as well. Clubs teams who do not include all groups of swimmers in training but instead cater to one or two fast swimmers will struggle to find team success. TEAM concepts must include all swimmers at any level not just the athletes at the top. By selfishly coaching only the select few swimmers at the top coaches are not inspiring success for the whole team. By including all swimmers, parents, and coaches TEAM culture creates a strong bond between all involved which cannot be broken.

Nobody on a team is better than anybody else including the coach. Why do the same teams always seem to win? Pursuing excellence boils down to everyone on the team believing and supporting each other. The support is led by the coach and trickles down to every team athlete and parent. College football is a great example. In fact, take any team sport and you will probably find the same result. A select few successful teams at the top, playing as a team. Yet I still see swimming programs that do not demand excellence for the whole team.

Having great success with Meyerland, I felt the need to move on to Space City Aquatic Team (SCAT) located in South Houston. At the time SCAT was an up and coming team training in two high school pools and one long course pool in the summer. Great coaching by head coach John Pittington led SCAT to place second at TAGS. I took an instant liking to the quick success SCAT had achieved, even though facilities were somewhat lacking. After meeting with the head coach, I accepted the Head Age Group Coaching position. By infusing concepts of Team I had been using thus far to SCAT we won three consecutive state championships, as well as placing swimmers at Junior and Senior Nationals. As the coaches, swimmers, and parents rallied together SCAT became stronger and stronger. We won as a team, each person depending on one another to accomplish our goal; to be the best, not as one but together. A pattern of success had been established.

To be brief, my swimming "career" started somewhere around age 7. At a local community pool, one of the summer league coaches saw potential in me splashing around and suggested I join the team. I quickly accelerated in the sport and, at my very first summer league championship, one of the year-round coaches scouting the talent nick-named me "super fly" and asked me to join his team. He was the head coach and I knew I was not going to be swimming with him for quite some time, but I decided to give it a shot. Each group that I moved through was progressively more difficult, but with that effort came success. Within a year, I was swimming with Coach John Vogel: a mean, chewing tobacco John Wayne type who swam for Tennessee. That man sure scared me and he did NOT accept excuses. This was 1979 at Space City Aquatic Club. In less than 2 years, our small team, against all odds, won the Texas Age Group Swimming Championship (TAGS). It all started when Coach Vogel walked into practice with a large funeral wreath and said that the wreath was sent to us by a team favored to win TAGS this year—little did we know, Coach Vogel bought the wreath himself. This single act got our whole team so fired up that we were going to do everything possible to win the meet as the underdogs. The other 3 boys on my relay team and I shaved our heads and we set the 10&under National Record for the 200 Medley Relay. We only held that record for about a week, but that night we were the kings. I know that John does not want this book to be about him, but without him, there was never any team. It was Coach Vogel's tenacity and stubbornness that kept us moving forward and training hard. As ankle biters, we always tried to get out of hard sets by feigning that we were going to throw up and asked to be excused to the bathroom. That only happened once as John would just bring the trash can over to us filled with his chewing tobacco spit and tell us to join him, but we better NOT miss the interval. I vividly remember being devastated when

John told our group that he was going to be taking a head coach position in north Houston in a little city called The Woodlands. We all, including our parents, pitched in and bought him a briefcase and filled it with Red Man tobacco and wished him well. I continued to swim for SCAT for a little while and then tried a team called STOP, but it just wasn't the same as training with John. To this day, I am not entirely sure how this happened, but after about 18 months of swimming for SCAT and STOP, my dad told me that we were going to start driving to The Woodlands to start swimming for John again!!!! I truly could not believe it, but my dad got off of work early (by going into work extra early) and braved Houston traffic every afternoon and Saturday mornings for several months to make sure I could swim with Coach Vogel. I would do my homework on the way to practice and sleep that whole way home because John's practices never got easier—in fact, they were much harder. When the school year ended, my dad got a new job in downtown Houston and we had the opportunity to move to The Woodlands. The very first summer that I lived in The Woodlands, we hosted and won TAGS. I was technically still unattached, but I was definitely a part of the Team. The opening night, we poured green dyed water into all the lanes after walking out to the loudspeakers playing Eye of The Tiger. Over the next several years, John continued to foster the team mentality by having team meetings, movie nights that had the whole team basically renting out the theater: watching Rocky 4, and watching the short film Godzilla versus Bambi short film before our championship meet…watch it on YouTube, you'll thank me! Swimming is definitely an individual sport in which most people become successful by having other individuals training just as hard as you do which pushes you to be better, but it is also very much a team sport because you are right there in the thick

John Vogel

of it with your teammates, and at the head of every great swimmer and team is its fearless leader, men like John Vogel. After high school, I swam in college for a few years, but it was never the same and I lost the drive to swim; however, I never forgot the lessons taught to me by John and the team. I used all that I learned and went to medical school and became an anesthesiologist. Ending back up to practice medicine in The Woodlands, John and I were reunited, and it was like we had never missed seeing each other despite it having been 20 years. John and I remain close friends, I've even done his anesthesia, and we usually take about once a month just catching up on life. I was with him when he was inducted into the Texas Swimming and Diving Hall of Fame and then again last year when The Woodlands Swim Team, our team, was inducted. That team taught me more about life than swimming and if any one of us ever had a problem, all of us would be there to support the other—just like our coach, John Vogel, always has and always will.

—BRYAN CLIFTON
Former SCAT and TWST swimmer

THE WOODLANDS—THE BEGINNING

In the summer of 1981 I was offered the head coaching position at The Woodlands Swim Team. Taking this position at The Woodlands scared me to death. I had my beliefs about TEAM, but now I had a choice; follow popular coaching philosophy or follow my heart. The obvious choice I did not have to think about was to follow my heart not the current trends. Taking my past knowledge of TEAM from my past swimming and coaching experiences, I started my journey at The Woodlands. Thinking back from summer league to Meyerland, to SCAT, we won. My goal was to lead The Woodlands

Swim Team in the same direction.

My start at The Woodlands was rough. First, a group of swimmers with no discipline or idea for how to be successful. Secondly, an assistant coach who did not like me. I knew I wanted a winning and successful team, but the only way to get there was for everyone else to want the same goal. I remembered a phrase from a movie I had watched, "cowboy up." This was my time to cowboy up and build a team.

After everyone completed the 3,000 meter butterfly workout assigned that first day; I instructed them to go home to rest and decide if they wanted to win as a team. To my shock, a changed group of swimmers showed up on the pool deck the next day. A team was born that first practice through adversity when they started to believe in each other. The second practice was great and the team was on the journey to becoming one. This was the start of Team at The Woodlands. I often reflect back to the midnight workout I had endured as a freshman at the University of Tennessee, where we as a team, had to "cowboy up" to complete that practice and support each other to finish it. When everyone is committed to achieving greatness the hard work of building a team can begin. Two years later we won our first of what would be twenty-six Texas Age Group State Championships. Winning traditions do not just happen. Winning takes hard work, dedication, a desire to achieve, respect, and supporting each other. These are the ingredients for Team.

John Vogel

Chapter 18

ENDINGS, BEGINNINGS, THE DASH

*This is a shirt signed and given to John
by past and current swimmers.*

When I retired from coaching The Woodlands Swim Team, I believed I would never coach again. I could not imagine wearing another team's colors which felt like I was betraying the team I loved and made part of my life for eighteen years. But once the coaching itch returned I realized that although I would always treasure my time at The Woodlands. I was still destined to be a swim coach.

When I finally realized the concept of TEAM had worked with all ability levels of athletes, I wanted to share the concept with other teams and individuals. I began speaking at coaching clinics, but my focus as well as my heart still wanted to work one on one with competitive swimmers who wanted to be the best they could be. Working with these athletes I was able focus on those who truly wanted to achieve and do what it takes to achieve success.

I have had some hard conversations with both swimmers as well as parents. I generally listen to the swimmer more than the parent. Most of the time a coach will learn quickly whether the swimmer wants to only participate or commit to excellence. For myself, participation means taking up lane space: do we as coaches give up on these individuals? Absolutely not. It is a coach's job to teach and encourage these swimmers to success. Now here is the beautiful part as well as the guts of this book. If these athletes can be convinced they have value and can contribute to the team's success, the coach has done his job. The team will win, but more importantly you will have helped swimmers to reach their full potential. "There is no I in team" as long as coaches, parents and swimmers embrace concepts of TEAM. I believe both teams as well as individuals will advance to the highest possible level. Creating the proper environment will enhance success while producing incredible results.

I hope this book will make a difference and help coaches, swimmers and teams have a higher level of success. The concepts of TEAM were compiled over many years with many people pulling together for a common goal. The achievements of teams I have coached were not based on a single coach or a swimmer but a group of dedicated people. No one person on a team is better than anyone else including the coaches. By letting go of egos and standing together as one, a team will achieve success. Learning to improvise, adapt, and overcome challenges is key. Much like in the military or a business, assess the situation and be flexible to try different ways to inspire success. More than anything else, believe in yourself and your team.

John Vogel, Nathan Adrian, and Jacob Gonzales at a local swim clinic.

Several years ago I spoke at a clinic for a large USA swim team in Texas. I wanted to try something new to inspire this team to do great things. I had recently come across the poem The Dash by

Linda Ellis. I find this poem inspirational as well as meaningful. This poem is most often read during funerals, but I feel the meaning of this poem can inspire greatness anytime. I decided to try visual techniques and use the poem to spark the importance of being the best you can be in life and swimming.

For this exercise, the swimmers were to lay on their backs while I turned the lights off. I asked them to picture a cemetery, and in particular a headstone. I went around the room touching the shoulders of some of the swimmers. As I touched their shoulder they were to tell me what they saw on that headstone. The first swimmer replied the dates of birth and death. The second swimmer I tapped on the shoulder answered with the person's name. Finally the third swimmer answered with something nice about the person and rest in peace. All were right answers, yet no one answered what the most important thing written on the stone was. The Dash between the dates. The dash represents the life someone lives between birth and death. It is the accomplishments or failures that happen while we are on this earth. The people we touch and life experiences that influence who we are as a person. I asked the swimmers to think about how they wanted to be remembered. Were they a hard worker, a good example for others, or a future good mother or father? You only get one dash in life, make the best of yours. How do you want to be remembered?

I would like to give a huge thank you to my assistant, Melissa Mathews Shimp. You would not be reading this book if not for Melissa's involvement in the writing and production of TEAM. I am going to leave you with a quote from legendary football coach Lou Holtz,

"There is never a right time to do the wrong thing, there is never a wrong time to do the right thing."

Learn to swim fast unshaven and above all believe…TEAM.

TO THE WOODLANDS SWIM TEAM PAST, PRESENT AND FUTURE:

This book is for all teams, but this page is dedicated to all the past, current, and future swimmers of The Woodlands Swim Team. I treasure my years with The Woodlands Swim Team and will always feel proud of the team's accomplishments. We were more than Team, we were a family.

To the current Woodlands Swim Team coaches and swimmers… Train together as one, trust each other, establish traditions, and win as a team. Your individual success will take care of itself. The current head coach Chris Collier has the team going in the right direction to succeed.

John and Chris Collier, current TWST Head Coach

To the past Woodlands Swim Team swimmers, you are what inspired this book. Your team is now your family, career, and anything else in your life which requires working together. Always remember what you accomplished as a team, apply it to your life, and you will achieve success. I love you guys.

Made in the USA
Coppell, TX
14 August 2021

60489092R00081